INTELLIGENCE
IN POLITICS

*The University of North Carolina Press, Chapel Hill, N. C.;
The Baker and Taylor Co., New York; Oxford University Press,
London; Maruzen-Kabushiki-Kaisha, Tokyo; Edward Evans &
Sons, Ltd., Shanghai.*

INTELLIGENCE
IN POLITICS

An Approach to Social Problems

BY

PAUL W. WARD

Author of *Sovereignty;* co-author of *The Fields
and Methods of Knowledge*

CHAPEL HILL
THE UNIVERSITY OF NORTH CAROLINA PRESS
1931

To

JOHN DEWEY

ἡ μὲν γὰρ ἐμπειρία τέχνην ἐποίησεν, ὡς φησὶ
Πῶλος, ὀρθῶς λέγων, ἡ δ' ἀπειρία τύχην.
ARISTOTLE, *Metaphysica*, 981 a 3.

FOREWORD

THE SOURCES of the ideas in the following chapters are widespread; some of them are common notions taken from forgotten contexts. The sharp emphasis on centralization and responsibility in social affairs derives from a street-corner conversation with Professor W. P. Montague as well as from a study of political history. My chief indebtedness is to Professor John Dewey; from him I have taken the emphasis on consequences and the general doctrine of the nature of intelligence.

The manuscript developed by a process of selection from lectures presented to my students. I have tried to use these points as pegs upon which to hang a social philosophy. Professor Harold A. Larrabee, of Union University, and Professor Frederick E. Lumley, of Ohio State University, have read the material in a previous form; Professor Hunley W. Herrington, of Syracuse University, has criticized the chapters in their present shape. I am grateful to all of these for their help. Thanks are due to the editors of *Social Forces* for permission to reprint that part of Chapter V which appeared in their journal for October, 1930.

P. W. W.

School of Citizenship and Public Affairs
Syracuse University, Syracuse, N. Y.
July 28, 1931

TABLE OF CONTENTS

TABLE OF CONTENTS

INTELLIGENCE
IN POLITICS

Chapter I

INSTITUTIONS AND INSTITUTIONAL CHANGE

THESE ARE DAYS of disenchantment. The "debunking" not only of personalities but of institutions proceeds apace. All the old heroes and conventions must look to their laurels; tradition is on the defensive.

However one may feel about it, the rate of social and intellectual change has greatly accelerated, although this change is not merely in one direction. Historically the medieval Church and the pioneer family have decayed, while machine industry, the modern state, and now a new international order, have emerged. If the history of the present age resembles that of previous periods it will be recorded that our current culture was characterized both by dissolution and by restless, explosive growth.

But who can be certain at such close range as to which is which? When the old landmarks are disappearing how can we expect any agreement of opinion? Speed obscures direction. The present is always an age of confusion.

At no point is the current criticism of existing institutions more pungent than in political affairs.

3

Traditional democratic theory wears its crown uneasily. The sovereign citizen of revolutionary thinking senses a loss of authority. He knows that some countries, such as Italy, have abandoned democratic government. Can it be that *vox populi* is no longer *vox dei?* A host of writers, among them Mr. Walter Lippmann, has assured him that "the assumption that either the voters are inherently competent to direct the course of affairs or that they are making progress toward such an ideal" is false.[1] According to Mr. Lippmann, to try to make the citizen omni-competent is as irrational as to try to make a fat man into a ballet dancer.

So the democratic citizen has come to feel like a child who has been tricked out of a bag of candy. He is a trifle uncertain as to whether he has just been fooled for the first time or whether he has been fooled all the time and is just finding it out. Has he just become a "phantom," or has he always been a ghost? Has democracy always been as unworkable as its critics now maintain, or has it become so only recently? Or is it really unworkable? Perhaps the citizen is not fooled after all. How, in these days of propaganda and psychoanalysis, can one be certain even that one has not systematically hoodwinked

[1] *The Phantom Public,* p. 38.

4

oneself? Although the writers on public opinion have vowed that the sum total of political wisdom is to "kid" and to be "kidded," could it not be that they, too, have fooled themselves?

Not only is the mind of the average citizen confused, but in the discussions of supposed experts political theory is very much tangled. To read current literature in the field is to realize that the varieties of opinion are such as to make possible an indefinite number of classifications. Writers differ as to the proper functions and probable developments of every human institution. They disagree almost as widely even as to the meanings of such terms as *institution*. Some find subtle distinctions among the terms *community, association,* and *institution;*[2] others deny even the existence of such things as the proper subject-matter of social science.[3] Each writer must be taken in terms of his own meanings to be intelligible. One will say that constitutional democracy has *a priori* validity;[4] another asserts that the current belief in democracy is itself a hindrance to political progress.[5] The time-honored quarrel between judges and legislators, a quarrel at

[2] R. M. MacIver, *The Modern State,* p. 6.
[3] F. H. Allport, in *American Political Science Review,* XXI, 611 f.
[4] W. Y. Elliott, *The Pragmatic Revolt in Politics.*
[5] John Dickinson, in *American Political Science Review,* XXIV, 287.

least as old as the days of Sir Edward Coke, has raised its head to add to the confusion. The lawyers have taken the legislators on the flank by capitalizing the current dissatisfactions with legislative bodies. They assert that judges have as much right to make law as have legislators[6] and that administrative officers must be increasingly responsible to the courts for the proper performance of their true functions.[7] Contrasting to this are movements for the popular recall of judges and the legislative review of judicial decisions. Some observers have been so overcome by the complexities of social and political affairs as to hold that silence is the best policy. Rather than speak falsely, or tell the unpleasant truth, they would say nothing at all.

To be silent is to adopt inaction as a policy. Useful changes are not usually facilitated by a policy of inaction. It is better to risk saying something false than to say nothing at all. Furthermore, the complications may not be so great as the apparent divergencies of opinion indicate. The law of parsimony should have a place in social science. Are there not, indeed, some simple obvious points of reference from which a survey of social matters may be expedi-

[6] Hugo Krabbe, *The Modern Idea of the State.*
[7] Leon Duguit, *Law in the Modern State.*

tiously begun, some statements as to subject-matter, methods, aims, or criteria which, when stated clearly, may claim immediate acceptance? It is the belief of the present writer that there are a few elementary distinctions which can be of great value in clearing up the ambiguities of current social thinking. These seem to be worth repeating, even at the risk of being trite or of adding another divergency to those already existing. All of the distinctions with which we shall be concerned have to do with the nature of human activity and with the business of human intelligence in social affairs.

INSTITUTIONS AS HUMAN CONDUCT

To begin with there is the distinction of the sub-ject-matter, the general characterization of the area in which the analysis of social science takes place. With what does social science begin? One would think that here, at the very start, no difference of opinion would be possible. As a matter of fact it is at the very beginning that the differences of opinion are both sharpest and most important, for the be-ginnings determine the direction of all the subse-quent analysis.

Traditionally social and political science has been too static. It has assumed social structures and then given an anatomical account of them. Historically it was undoubtedly important that it be recognized that there were such things as social organizations. The analysis of their anatomy, however, furnished little clue to the curing of their ills; the expert in social structures proved to be as incompetent in social engineering as a mere expert in anatomy is in therapeutics. It is the *activity* which is important. Indeed, the significant object of attention in all of the sciences is movement; how do things change, and what do they do, are questions asked about every sort of subject-matter. Activity is fundamental.

Furthermore, the activities which interest the social scientist are the functions of living beings. The activity is living activity, more like plant action than inorganic activity. Man is an animal, acting, living, doing in a shifting environment. This environment is itself active. Its activities are different in character from the functions of protoplasm, but only in terms of this environment does the organism live. Living organisms float in a context of environing movement. The movements of each living thing form part of the environment of other specific living things, as the other activities of an organism form part of the environment of any specific activity of that organism. Human organisms are but focal

8

centers among other activities, some human, some merely organic, and others inorganic in character.

The social scientist must take some account of these other activities as they affect those functions in which he is particularly interested. The physical activities of the environment will have a profound effect upon the development of human behavior and, where culture or civilization is rude and primitive, its influence will be preponderant. A tribe living on a small island in the tropics, or within the icy fastness of the polar regions, will exhibit in its adult activities a pattern reflecting the necessities of its physical environment. The biological environment is even more obviously important. The flora and fauna of an area condition in a very marked way the human activities which are parasitic upon them. But, where a high degree of civilization exists, the social environment is of paramount significance in the formation of the qualitative changes which appear in human conduct. Civilized man's original nature is identical with that of the aborigines, to all intents and purposes, but his adult life is very different indeed. In an educated occidental adult a great qualitative change has been grafted upon an original matrix of activity which is not greatly different from the original nature of an Australian

Bushman. The natural physical environment does not account for the change. In both cases the social equipment of the environment is crucial in the positive modification of human action.

In specific developments any of the environing activities may give a heavy over-stimulation to certain of man's activities and too little stimulation to others. Life can be only a terrified dream at the foot of an active volcano or in the bitter, decimating chill of a paleolithic glaciation. It is a dream, albeit a different one, to the monk in a monastery. Distortions of various kinds may result from the focusing of stimuli at certain spots. Not even history exhausts the possible vagaries of human conduct. Geography and climate play a large part, but to reflect five minutes upon the anthropological contributions to social science is to realize that, however important inorganic activities may be, the natural science which furnishes the chief basis for social thinking is biology. Below the level of this science the social scientist goes infrequently and then with the same motives which animate the biologist.

In brief, social scientists are interested in activity, in human activity, which is best thought of as a body of living functions within a background of other activities. But they are not interested in all human activities. One way of indicating the distinct phases of activity which interest the student of society is to employ the terms *behavior* and *conduct*. Bare *activity* is mere movement, relocation in space. *Behavior* is a certain kind of activity; it is adaptive activity. Plants and animals behave. *Conduct* is a term even more restricted in its denotation; it refers to *socially significant action*. We observe behavior, but we also approve and disapprove conduct. The subject-matter of social science is conduct; but conduct is also behavior. It is because of this fact that a systematic approach to social science should begin with reference to the characteristics shared by both behavior and conduct. Social science assumes, therefore, such biological and psychological distinctions as organism and environment, native and acquired characteristics, original activities and conditioned responses, and all of the psychological description of habit-formation and the learning process.

Recently Mr. John Dewey has suggested that it is the fact of our being involved in the consequences of each other's acts which generates a "public."[8] A "public" is simply the body of persons concerned in

[8] John Dewey, *The Public and Its Problems*.

the results of some conjoint action. This is remarkably near the etymological meaning of the term *republic;* the *res publica* of the Romans was the body of action involving the most inclusive area of consequences. Within such an area there may be an indefinite number of smaller groupings, as diminutive wave-motions may fall within larger ones when concentric circles spread from the falling of stones into a lake.

Taking this definition, social science is simply the study of *socially significant* bodies of action. The fact that we are involved in the consequences of our various conjoint actions gives human behavior the quality we call *social* and makes possible social science. Mr. Dewey's distinction of the nature of the public cuts the Gordian knot; the problem is not one of a fictitious "common will," or of a "group mind," or some other intangible and mythological entity; but the whole matter of social science is merely the distinguishing of actions which involve others in their consequences, direct and indirect, and a deliberate attempt to take care of those consequences. All the multitudinous forms of social organization which history displays are but the blundering attempts, mostly failures, of men to handle their mutual conduct.

INSTITUTIONAL CHANGE

Indeed, when men began to write history, human behavior had already various patterns which were changing in response to the play of the unconscious forces of man's nature and its environment. Human conduct in the primitive stage had to meet the inimical play of natural selection. Natural forces beat upon emerging man with the same relentlessness which they displayed toward all other life. Only forms with resourcefulness and flexibility survived the various selective ordeals of primitive conditions.

Human activity is, of course, similar to other life. Certain centers of energy appear in contrast to a more or less homogeneous background. Divergent structures make possible divergent acts. A division of labor, a specialization of function, is to be noted in human conduct and, at any level, this must be sufficient to prevent the elimination of the total body of supporting action. Natural selection is negative. So long as any particular body of action does not actually kill its supporting activity, by sabotaging it in such a way as to occasion its submergence in the struggle for existence, there is no natural selection operative. The environment, moreover, is at least as tolerant of vagaries of cultural pattern as it is of chromosomal aberrations and gene mutations. Consequently not all institutions, either primitive or modern, are necessarily useful biologically; the fact that a certain pattern exists is no reason for assuming that there is no better way in which the particular stock of action may become organized.

Changes are constantly taking place in the institutions of every society, from various causes and with varying rates of speed. When pressure is put upon any stock of activity the inefficient and inadequate organizations tend to give way. Pressure from without sets up realignments of institutions within a total stock of activity. Invasions, migrations, wars, famines, and plagues twist and divert the habits of men in peculiar ways. Variations of nature and of inventiveness produce other alterations. Distortions produced either by external or internal agencies may become habitual and subsequently may be regarded as indispensable parts of particular cultures. Highly artificial and effete institutions, as judged by exterior standards, may seem to the people who *live* them to be very "natural," and even inevitable, so long as their consequences are not unendurable.

The consequences of institutions, however, cannot be forever ignored. Frequently, indeed, they are aimed at deliberately. A society with any degree of intelligence will have some kind of social knowledge. It would not be true to say that institutions always aim at results; for *aim* implies a conscious intention. Genuine social science is both rare and recent. The habits of men are more blind than intelligent. Human habits are today what they are, not as the result of reflection exclusively, but chiefly because of a long series of biological, anthropological, and historical accidents. The social storms and stresses, the care and neglect, of all previous ages of men have left their imprint upon the existing bodies of human habit. Social institutions have their various factors, some useful, others harmful, and still others neutral, even as the human body has its strong, its weak, and its neutral features. Furthermore, the habits of society have vestigial functions within them which may be compared to the vestigial organs of the human body.

The pattern of human activity, however, is more readily changed than are the organs of the human body. It may seem, at times, as though this were not the case. But the physical machinery of contemporary man is identical, biology tells us, with that of neolithic man of twenty-five thousand years ago. Our habits, by contrast, are different from those of neolithic culture to a degree which tempts one to use the word *total*. The changes which have come have been unconscious, however, rather than premeditated. Men here and there have seen what they were doing, and social inventiveness has flourished in certain fortunate periods of history, notably in ancient Greece, but to maintain that the habits of men today are predominantly the results of reflective invention and that they are, therefore, the best possible, would be both to over-intellectualize history and to calumniate intelligence. Nevertheless, they have changed and are changing with an acceleration which startles the timid.

In the absence of a highly-developed social knowledge, with the average mind largely ignorant both of what is done and of what might be done, social changes are matters of *toleration* on a plane which is, for the most part, sub-reflective. In primitive groupings, human habits might endure, although progressively more and more ill-adapted to the environment and to each other, until the group was eliminated; animal forms can tolerate anything, excepting only death. But, as sensitivity increases, the toleration of antique habits, merely because they are habits, decreases. Higher forms of human society are forms in which the toleration point is well above that required for mere biological existence; a certain minimum amount of goods and services has come to be demanded by all. Today we know better than merely to subsist. Popular education is increasing enlightenment, after a fashion, and decreasing the toleration felt toward old habits by the average man. We know more, and stand for less merely because it is old, than did our ancestors. The development of thought as a social device has changed social affairs from being questions of what man can biologically *endure* to matters of what he is reflectively willing to *tolerate*.

The whole of social development might be treated as the progressive decrease of unreflective endurance in this sense; or to state it the other way around, the emergence of reflective knowledge. The simple fact has been that increasing environmental complexities have so involved and confused the earlier patterns of human conduct that they have been forced by successive conflicts into reorganization after reorganization as intelligence developed. Reflection has now reached such a point in human life that man not only turns to it to help himself out of his intolerable existing predicaments but also, in terms of it, attempts to discount future difficulties. Some men definitely avoid future clashes as a result of recognizing that the only way to prevent them is to take precautions here and now.

The rise of social science marks the deliberate attempt by men consciously to evaluate their social habits. It is the preliminary to social engineering on a scale analogous to the engineering we now have in physical, chemical, and biological science. Our habits, our institutions, are certain ways of getting things done. Scientific criticism of them should make clear to us (1) *what, as a matter of fact, is done by the present forms of our conduct* and (2) *what the consequences of alternative methods of procedure would be.* If we wish to do again the things which previously have been done in these spheres of action, social science will tell us how to do them more rapidly and easily. If we wish to do other things, social science will guide the experiments which are to be undertaken. It is not extravagant to assert that a mature social science will engineer reforms which are not even dreamed of as possibilities today.

THE FUNCTION OF OFFICIALS

The bodies of action which we call institutions are guided by individual officers. An *official* of an institution is a person who devotes a large portion of his time to a particular class of actions in a supervisory or directive capacity. The one who assumes any official position, whether as a county clerk, a traffic officer, a club treasurer, or a state governor, transacts business which differs in character from the affairs of those who are not officials. The traffic officer may take his own automobile and drive it to his home; the county clerk, as a clerk, may issue to himself, as bachelor, a license to marry; the governor, as citizen, may obey his own administrative rulings; but the *official aspect* of their action is distinguishable from that portion which is homogeneous with the rest of the institution involved.

An office may be regarded as a pivot for the reorganization of conduct. It is a nexus of action by means of which a certain efficiency may be achieved and a certain control may be exercised. A constitution, in the words of Aristotle, is an organization of offices. It is an habitual arrangement of vantage points with reference to social actions, points through which men perform official acts, and which then pass on to other men without necessarily disturbing the social patterns of behavior. Where there is no habit, there can be no officers. Only institutions can have officials; they alone have that structural continuity necessary for scientific definition and analysis. They, as we have seen, are bodies of continued or recurrent conduct.

Suppose two bodies of activity come into conflict?

Part of the business of officials is to pilot the activities so that they do not crash into each other violently. But if the officials of two institutions come into conflict—two whole sets of activity, in other words? What then?

In the primitive forms of life, the intricacies of organization were relatively few; the patriarch was head-man of domestic, religious, economic, and ecclesiastical affairs. All quarrels were either against or among the elders. But, as the multiplicity of detailed groupings developed, severe inter-departmental conflicts became more unavoidable. For example, out of the welter of barbarism which followed the decline of Roman power two great groupings of activity emerged in Western Europe, the Church and the Empire. Each could settle conflicts within itself, so to speak; that is, its officials were supported by the mass of activity to the extent of exercising sufficient power to prevent violence. But between the two classes of action there developed a conflict of major proportions. It was a bitter quarrel, and one party had to lose irretrievably. All persons belonged to the Empire; all persons belonged to the Church. But the officials of the Church were not the officials of the Empire. So each man was split in two, and the two halves, through their official representatives, were fighting each other.

The intolerable character of the medieval conflict, even worse than that of most civil wars, was accentuated by the fact that there was no established machinery for peaceful adjustment. There was no way for these officials to come to terms excepting by mutual consultation. They, in the meantime, had forgotten the meaning of their official positions, and claimed an absoluteness which no official has ever enjoyed. There was no power above them to force them to their senses by saying to them that they should adjust their differences peacefully, or give up their offices to others who could. So they clutched each other's throats, and Western Europe suffered. But while they did this, the dapper young kings of national states saw their opportunity. They became gracious, solicitous, and benign. They sent out their publicity agents, as it were, and sold to the people of Western Europe absolute secular monarchy as the solution of their ills. It was with a distinct feeling of relief from an intolerable situation that men turned to the rising absolute monarchs of national states.

The moral of this little sketch of past history is that, where conflicts arise, there must eventually be adjusting machinery. Men cannot and will not go on forever bleeding internally from conflicts among interests all of which seem to them important. Officials who refuse to make tolerable arrangements find in the end that they are no longer officials; they forfeit their representative function, and new organizations of human activities, with new representatives, emerge.

At every level of human conduct such adjustments take place. The pluralism of the ethical goods of life demands adjustment. The activities of men are diverse. Some seek to do what others seek to prevent. Some wish to possess what others have and wish to retain. In the welter of conflicting means and ends, anarchy is avoided only by the erection of definite adjusting machinery. The difficulty is, of course, that official machinery which serves the purpose of adjustment well enough on one level requires in turn to be adjusted, at another level, to other similar machinery. This was the problem between the officials of medieval Church and Empire, and this is the difficulty among the governments of the modern states of Western Europe. Even when they are internally successful in their functions as adjusters of conflict they are in a state of anarchy with similar sets of officials in other territories.

The Testing of Institutions and Officials

All social institutions are, in fact, experimental. The ways in which certain ends are collectively achieved are tentative in that they are the transient forms taken by the community as it attempts, half-consciously, to guide itself. If we take the total body of action involved at any time as the *community,* then the institutions of that community are methods of procedure and its bodies of officials are *organs* of the collective action. These are always in flux; methods change, and officials both change in character as well as come and go in their representative capacities. The business of social science is to see that, in every case, they change for the better rather than for the worse, in terms of the consequences achieved. *Institutions are ways of achieving goods and services;* social science aims to improve both the goods and the services. The state, as Aristotle said long ago, continues in existence "for the sake of a good life." It is best regarded as an organization of public services. It, and every other institution, is to be criticized in terms of the quality and quantity of the goods and services it renders the community. And of this who, pray, is a better judge than the community itself? Courts of law have their part to play in holding institutional forms responsible for the transaction of their intended business, as M. Leon Duguit has insisted.[9] But courts are themselves organs of the community and are ultimately responsible to the community.

The extent to which any particular institution shall spread its control is also a matter for experiment, to be determined only by scientific analysis. Each social project has its own engineering difficulties. The extension of state functions, for example, has been traditionally opposed in terms of the assumption that private initiative is more effective than public enterprise.[10] Aristotle expressed this notion, in criticizing Plato, when he said everyone's business tends to become no one's business. Enterprises are so large nowadays, however, and are carried on to such a large degree by technical experts that there seems to be no antecedent reason why public enterprises should not be as effectively conducted as are private ones, however the case may have stood in previous times. The modern city, or state, can hire administrative officials and technicians as easily as can any privately managed business corporation. Projects of supreme moment, such as national defense, fall inevitably into the most direct

[9] See Paul W. Ward, *Sovereignty,* pp. 126 f.
[10] See Howard L. McBain, in *Whither Mankind* (editor, Chas. A. Beard), pp. 146-147.

control of the community through its government. Private management in control of any basic necessity by way of goods or services survives only at the price of increasing excellence in performance. Exploitation, or aggravated wastefulness by way of competition on the part of large corporations handling important services, immediately raises the question of the expediency of annexing their administration to existing institutions already directly responsible to the community. There is no antecedent formula which can indicate accurately the extent to which direct public control either may or will be extended. The community decides, and from the decision of the community there is no appeal.

The same experimental test should be applied to specific officials. Where a body of action is directed by a particular man or woman, the desirability of the particular office-holder is to be determined by a critical analysis of the way in which the action is supervised and directed. The official aspect of the activity is to be criticized, and its quality alone signifies the value of the official to the institution concerned.

It is easy to say that we should make officials and institutions justify themselves by results and, if they do not bear inspection, demand new ones. But the difficulties in the way of such criticism are immense. It may appear that something is wrong, but whether it be particular men who should be displaced, or whole stocks of habit which must be altered, is not always apparent. The body of habit ebbs and flows, and officials come and go; changes in minute detail, as well as in official personnel, occur in every institution. The scene is constantly shifting. If something is wrong, who or what is to blame?

In the past the dislocation, deliberate and otherwise, which accompanied the emergence of a novel institution was usually so large in amount and so confused in character that many generations might be involved before a new equilibrium definitely appeared. Social science, if it were adequate, would enable men today to make changes deliberately and immediately; precise scientific knowledge of what is the matter and of whom to blame is a necessary preface to intelligent action. It is interesting to note the technique which has been worked out in political affairs to provide for the progressive criticism both of personnel and of policies.

Chapter II

THE MEANING OF DEMOCRACY

THE NEED FOR centralization and for the elimination of the internal conflicts which men felt at the end of the Middle Ages was met by the development of the absolute monarchy. No large political structure is effective which is not centralized administratively. This need for effectiveness was met by defining the monarch as *sovereign*. He was given the supreme control, apotheosized into an authority reminiscent of the Roman Emperor. The antidote to the anarchy of medievalism was power, centralized, secular, absolute, and irresponsible. The sovereign of the modern state was representative of his people but not responsible to them, nor subject to their control, apart from revolution. Men saved themselves from anarchy by a worship of uncontrolled power.

POLITICAL DEMOCRACY

It soon became apparent, however, that uncontrolled power issued in tyranny. To focus power apart from responsibility is to organize oppression; to focus responsibility apart from power is to make scapegoats. The problem was to focus both executive control and responsibility in the same offices.

27

The solution hit upon was the ballot—the election of officials by the system called representative government.

The essence of this scheme of organization is that, at stated intervals, or under specified conditions, the officials of the political structure come before the judgment of those who make up that structure. The assumption is that *those who take the consequences of public policy should pass upon it* by approving or rejecting those officials who administer public affairs, or who wish to do so. Democratic government is, consequently, *institutionalized responsibility in public office.* The organization of secular power had been the antidote to anarchy; the organization of responsibility has been attempted as the cure for the arbitrary abuse of power.

The seventeenth century in England saw the emergence of this rough test for political officials. Since then it has spread to various other countries and to some other institutions. *Wherever all those who take the consequences of policy have a safeguarded veto upon policies and personnel, there may be said to be democracy.* Industry and higher education, to mention only two classes of action, are spheres into which this technique of responsibility has spread very slowly. The typical executive in higher education is responsible to a board of trustees, or regents, who do not take the direct consequences of changes of policy and whose opinions pro and con are, therefore, only accidentally useful. Only indirect consequences affect them. In business the executive is responsible, for the most part, only to the capital invested; the stockholders who elect the directors are investors. The workers are not asked to vote upon either personnel or policy. The employees, however, take the consequences of changes of policy even more obviously than do the investors in industry.

The organization of responsibility, in other words, is not a simple matter. It may be worked out fairly well in some spheres and not at all in others. Even where the machinery seems to be available the difficulties are very great. How, for example, in political matters can one be sure that a particular official is competent, or is working with a definite policy in any particular direction? Our enterprises are large, and officials become remote. A policy, be it noted, is a systematic series of aimed-at consequences. In order to be criticized, policies must exist, of course, and be precisely defined. The best of officials will make mistakes; but unless there is a specific policy, we cannot always tell whether a mistake has been made or not. The worst of all policies is to have no policy. "Muddling through" is the perennial and intolerable crime of officialdom. All that can be done by an observer is to infer from the public actions of the official concerned the consequences at which he is aiming. "Handsome is as handsome does." Our criticism of officials may be largely based, in obscurer moments, upon mere conjecture. Indeed, the *chief problem of democratic government is to organize effective public criticism of officials in terms of their policies.*

Here appears the value of such suggestions as the one frequently made in reference to the cabinet secretaries of the government of the United States. These secretaries should be brought into the sessions of Congress, to be questioned upon their policies, and should sit in all sessions as participants, as do the government ministers in the English House of Commons. In this way the policies of the government would receive a more detailed and intelligent criticism than is possible at present, both by legislators and, through newspaper reports, by the public. As matters now stand, only by an investigating committee can cabinet secretaries be brought before members of either the Senate or the House. An investigating committee is, of course, all too frequently a political *post mortem*. At best a retrospective responsibility can be organized, whereas progressive criticism would make possible a greater responsiveness to public opinion. Not only would ill-advised policies be checked, but suggestions for policy might be gained from sources now unutilized. At all events, weaklings could not survive as cabinet officials in the face of such public criticism as the suggested change contemplates, and a premium would be placed upon high-grade executives in these important ministerial positions. This consequence alone would justify the change—a change necessitated only because of the ruling of an early President. The quarrels of early American politicians ought not to be allowed to cripple the political technique of a great state.

In general, the two principles, (1) *centralization of authority,* and (2) *the focusing of responsibility,* are valuable guides in the reconstruction of institutional activities. No official can be held responsible for consequences which are beyond his control, nor can those who are to blame for bad consequences be known unless authority be centralized. In ordinary procedure the focusing of authority is as much a matter of fixating a *definite* structure for criticism as it is the insistence upon efficiency. Of course, too great administrative centralization may produce congestion; but too great definiteness in official spheres is impossible. As we have said, a policy which is bad can be known as such only when it has been defined. No goal can be either missed or achieved where none is involved.

The problem of organizing authority and responsibility is met with *at every level* of social life. If anything is to be done there must be specialization in performance; and those designated for specific rôles significant enough to criticize and to control, do well in their various parts, or they do not. They are, therefore, to be retained in their respective capacities, or others should be selected to carry on their functions. The problem is not merely political, but is present in all classes of social action—clubs, churches, schools, and industries, as well as at all levels of political activity.

Democratic theory has been severely criticized recently, as we have mentioned. Current psychology has pointed out that man's nature is primarily active, passionate, or impulsive, rather than intelligent. All current interpretations of human motivation discount the supposed automatic rationality of man's nature assumed by eighteenth-century philosophy. Most people, the argument runs, do not know what they want, and it is impossible to tell them what they want. Does this mean that there is no hope after all? Because the average man does not know his own best interests, are we to give up the attempt to control social affairs?

Some have thought so. To the rationalistic assumptions of traditional democratic political theory, contemporary psychology has dealt a cruel blow. We are not rational after all; how then, shall we govern ourselves? Public opinion is but the organization of prejudice. A large amount of the theorizing which has gone in terms of the "common will" of Rousseau has turned out to be false. The average man does not know the issues as do those who are the responsible leaders of a group. He never has so known them. Does this mean that democracy is a failure, and that we must lapse into aristocratic forms of control in social affairs?

Not by any means. The discovery that the average man is no more stupid than he is ought to be a source of satisfaction. Even though modern science is still in its infancy, it seems fair to assume that the average level of intelligence in any considerable block of the population of occidental society is well above that of any preceding century. Furthermore, psychology has not pointed out the *impossibility* of knowledge, but merely the scarcity of it.

In human nature there are unused potentialities which have been revealed along with the habit and the blind impulsiveness which are so frequently urged as refutations of democratic theory. In fact *there is no alternative but to assume the possibility of a consciously self-directed society.* Everything else in the way of government has been tried and has failed. Of course, no one expects every citizen of the United States to know precisely whether the Indians are properly cared for, whether the Bertillon system of criminal identification is usefully employed, or what are the technical dimensions of the service types of aircraft in the Army and Navy. But the general public must be consulted on the major issues; the whole bulk of action involved takes the consequences of public policy and it, therefore, should be ultimately the dictator of policy. The problem is to make it articulate. In the enforcement of law it is notorious that the bulk of the community action must be behind an enactment, or it will not be enforceable. In all public legislation and administration, the total bulk of action must support the policies adopted. In the face of a failure of such support, minorities can continue to govern only at the risk of revolution.

The question is not whether democracy is a brilliant success, but whether any other form of social control has a chance of doing better. When faced with this alternative, it seems inevitable that the possibility of democratic self-government be assumed, if only for the reason that all the arguments about the irrationality and prejudice of human nature apply with equal force to the self-appointed dictators and aristocrats who would be leaders of the "unwashed herd" in an undemocratic society. The total body of action, stupid as it may be on a specific issue, stands to lose rather than to gain by deliberately turning over the reins of control to the private passions of a select group. Mankind, as Mr. Dewey has pointed out, has suffered more from "leaders" who have had the power to harm than it has from the masses.

Democracy is not a faith; it is a policy. As such it is to be tested by its consequences. Sufficient of the consequences are available to indicate that the stability and orderliness of social structure which is essential to the intelligent development of the further goods and services of an enjoyable life are facilitated by common participation in the selection of specific policies as well as the common sharing of their consequences. Where the few select and the many endure, irresponsibility is encouraged on the part of both, and a decay of the self-conscious community results. "Self-government is better than good government," because the former is an indispensable condition of the latter.

There are no insuperable difficulties in the theory of a consciously self-controlled society. Its difficulties are those of the organization of intelligence, a problem which is faced in any event. The fact of specialization is no refutation of democratic political theory; the Greek criticisms do not hold. We do not select admirals in the Navy by lots. The democratic life is the achievement of an organization of specializations; again, a problem which must be faced in any event. *Those who take the consequences of policies should choose policies.* This is the basic proposition of democracy. This was the meaning of the Revolutionary cries "No taxation without representation!" "Government by consent of the governed!"

MAKING THE PUBLIC ARTICULATE

The problem of organizing democratic social control is to provide the scientific machinery for making the total mass of action consciously self-directing.

Genuine self-government, as contrasted to "muddling through" will come only with the development of improved facilities for providing the public with enlightening digests of the anticipated consequences of the alternative courses of action with reference to which their judgment is necessarily consulted. Here we need scientific inventiveness, downright creative genius. If astronomy demands a two-hundred-inch eye in order that its business go on, if biology demands more and more powerful microscopes as an extension of its eyes, it seems plausible that social science should be allowed to claim a little of our inventive attention in carrying on its experiments and investigations. Certainly issues are at stake which are as important to us as the nature of spiral nebulae and of the mechanism of heredity.

The technical organization of intelligence in social matters has not been achieved on a mass-production basis. For that reason democratic institutions have often become the football of special interests. Formal education of the population is not enough, although the heightened sensitiveness to public policy which is in evidence today seems for the most part to be a reflection of it. A society cannot be better than its system of education, and even the finest technical training will not provide one with the current alternatives of policy which may demand decision. One of the most bewildered classes of the population is composed of the college graduates. They feel that they ought to know what to do, and yet they know that they are, in fact, as ignorant of the specific issues as those less fortunate in educational opportunities. The facts and the contrasting theories must be presented in organized and digested form for the enlightment of the public; otherwise self-guidance is impossible.

In the recent past current issues were discussed only by "stump" speeches, such as the Lincoln-Douglas debates of the American Civil War period. The Greek city-state, according to Aristotle, was of ideal size when it did not exceed in numbers those who could be seen at a single view and reached by the sound of a single voice. Speech-making was the only technique of public deliberation. There has been more progress in this matter of organizing public opinion since the Lincoln-Douglas debates than there was in the entire period from the Periclean Age to 1860.

The daily newspaper has developed most conspicuously. Although still in its infancy as a means of enlightenment, the press has become so powerful that we frequently hear the phrase "government by newspaper." Much of the power of the press is adventitious and comes not so much from the editorial expression of opinion as from the deliberate bias used in the selection of news by which to divert public attention this way or that.[1] The importance of a professional ethics in this field, which will make for an unbiased recording of facts, is evident. A misstatement of fact on an important issue might well have attaching to it an overt penalty as severe as that for medical malpractice. If public enlightenment rests in the hands of editors, as public health is in the hands of the medical profession, the editor should be held accountable as well as the physician. Legal means are extreme measures, however; the more promising method of procedure is to encourage by every other available means the development of a self-conscious tradition in journalism analogous to the best research traditions of the first-class universities of the country. Journalism as a profession has a more and more important duty to civilization. In a day when we cannot talk matters over together—there are too many of us—we must be guided in a large measure by the printed page.

A new factor, however, has just entered the field.

---

[1] Such as the misrepresentation of the Russian Revolution by the *New York Times*. See supplement to the *New Republic* of August 4, 1920.

The Greek city-state with its orators, and the speech-making of a pioneer democracy are all obsolete in the face of the possibilities of radio transmission. Even the newspapers of our current industrialism are wondering what the radio will do to them. By radio the facts concerning important public affairs can be broadcast even while they are happening. Officials can be heard discussing matters of common concern more easily than was possible in the Greek city-state or the New England town meeting. Rival policies can be "put on the air" for the general public as they were, in part, in the last national presidential campaign in the United States. Here is a technique which can be indefinitely developed. In the English House of Commons it is customary to have questions answered by the ministers of the government; newspapers print the answers to these question the following day. What could be more to the point than to have the House, and all other important deliberative assemblies, assigned radio wave-lengths by which unobstructed transmissions of their sessions could be put on the air for the public ear? Both state and federal governments in the United States could be so reported. In the radio we have one of those key inventions, like the printing-press and the internal-combustion engine, which unlock a long series of new potentialities. It would be a gross tactical blunder for modern democratic civilization to abandon it to the exclusive use of the tooth-paste, cigarette, and automobile manufacturers.

It may be argued, of course, that the radio may be used as a means of propaganda, that the arguments concerning matters of policy may be broadcast with an adroitness and a falsity equal to that of the stump speech, the venal editorial, or the subsidized lobbyist. True enough. It is, as a matter of fact, too simple to trust to a technical contrivance which might turn out, if uncontrolled, to intensify all the old evils. Apart from the possibilities of propaganda, public deliberations suffer when their popular appeal is compared to matters of more dramatic interest. Who would care to listen in at a reading of the Congressional Record? Deliberative assemblies are rarely as thrilling as prize-fights and football matches. In times of crisis, however, nothing is more interesting than public policies. The radio is an instrumentality which intensifies our contact with each other. It is a means, therefore, which increases the possibilities both of vicious propaganda and of enlightenment. As such it intensifies the problem of the formation and development of opinion.

The Rôle of the Expert

How can expert opinion be made effective? This is the heart of the problem of democratic groups today. Such social knowledge as does exist must be brought to bear upon the points of uncertainty, where policies are forming which are of concern to the whole bodies of action involved. What is the rôle of the expert in a democracy? If the old systems are not adequate, certainly the expert should not preach the doctrinairism of antique politics. Nor, indeed, of antique morals. Mr. Lippmann's advocacy of *disinterestedness* in morals[2] is scarcely helpful to the selection of proper courses of action, either in private or public affairs. The cure of conflict is not in lack of interest. That way lies asceticism. There is, in fact, no single motive which is moral *per se,* as there is no single plan of social action which is always correct. It would be economical of thought if we could find formulas which would be forever trustworthy, but in ethical and political affairs history has demonstrated that to believe in such formulas is too fond. There is no short-cut. The hope of improvement in life in all its phases lies not in the inculcation of some single supposititious "moral" motive, nor in the achieving and memorizing of some system which

[2] In his *Preface to Morals.*

will supposedly guide us correctly, but in the development of intelligence and the making effective of it at the points where it can make a difference. In every crisis the alternative courses of action must be thought out; they must be dramatically portrayed and selected in terms of the best available scientific instruments of analysis.

The expert in social science, therefore, can help make the public, his fellows, articulate in reference to their matters of common interest by *stating concisely what is possible.* He can portray alternative courses of collective action, facilitating by this act the function of reflection and the selection of policies. *The people ought not to be consulted on matters of fact, but on those of desire, and they can desire intelligently only where the possibilities are revealed to them.* The expert's business is to reveal social possibilities; the people may then, by their votes or their representatives' votes, select, among the possibilities before them, the ends at which they wish to aim and the means the use of which they are willing to risk.

A group of experts has done this very thing recently in connection with the electric power industry in the United States. Mr. W. E. Mosher and his associates, in their book on *Electrical Utilities*,[3] have given in the first place an analysis of the present status of this industry, calling attention to its rapid growth, to the social importance of its service, to the fact that the present financial structures in the industry are without adequate public supervision owing to the breakdown of public service commissions. These commissions lack even a satisfactory basis for determining valuations for rate-making purposes. Then these writers have sketched certain possible methods of solving the problem presented, clearly defining alternative policies which may be adopted: (1) control through contracts made by the various states; (2) federal ownership of such power plants as Muscle Shoals and Boulder Dam, in order that an experimental basis for evaluation may be reached; (3) control by a league of municipalities as in the Canadian province of Ontario; (4) control by a National Planning Commission, similar to the Electricity Commission of 1919 or the Electricity Board of 1926 in England; and (5) control through national ownership. This is an excellent illustration of the function of expert opinion by way of revealing possible courses of action in a democratic society.

[3] *Electrical Utilities; The Crisis in Public Control,* by William E. Mosher, Editor; Finla G. Crawford, Ralph E. Himstead, Maurice R. Scharff, and Louis Mitchell.

The instrumentalities by means of which expertness may be brought to bear upon collective problems are many. Direct information to all concerned has been facilitated, as we have indicated, by the newspaper and the radio. Technical experts as permanent government officials advising legislative committees, as well as temporary councils of experts, are parts of every well-organized state using the invention of representative government. Any and every means of bringing the facts before the attention of those concerned should be exploited as the organization of intelligence proceeds.

Democracy *Versus* Revolution

Apart from a progressive, organized criticism of any section of human conduct, the method of social change must be eventually explosive. Where the complaints of those who represent the activities which are at a disadvantage, because of over-developments in other directions, cannot become articulate, deliberate redress is impossible. Either the repression of the activity becomes complete, or the pressure increases to the point of explosion. It is a fallacy, refuted by merely a cursory study of history, that "truth crushed to earth will rise again." Ways of thinking, even though superior, may be eliminated. It is also a fallacy to suppose that whole institutions may not be eradicated. Activities other than thinking are also open to coercion. But whenever the social pressure is not such as to eradicate, where annihilation is not complete, though attempted, or where stupidity and habit merely accidentally combine to produce stresses among activities, the social stage is set for revolution.

Revolutions are both interesting and illuminating. Invariably there are activities involved which are submerged or at a disadvantage in the organization of the particular institution or total social order. All groups within the state are, of course, presumably voluntary today, so that all revolutions are political in character; any group using violence as a weapon becomes political in its significance by virtue of that fact.

When a revolution is "brewing," the submerged, or excluded, activities, since they have no direct participation in affairs, effect an organization among themselves. Where a whole social order is under a small bureaucracy, as in Russia before the Revolution, or France before 1789, the bulk of the people's conduct is under pressure, and a condition of strain runs through the whole social structure. Occasional repressive acts of violence towards those who come, in specific accidental situations, to represent the submerged activities, aggravate the strain as well as give evidence of it. The causes of a revolution, all too frequently confused with the occasion of it, lie back in those preceding situations in which were produced the stresses and tensions which, in their release, produce such havoc. The dramatic event, or particular impact, which sets off the cataclysm throws little light on its nature and none upon its causes or consequences.

Only after a long series of social explosions, or revolutions, was representative government invented. It is essentially a device for making revolution unnecessary. By voting, the battles of possible revolutions are settled without bloodshed. Governments are changed in policies and personnel without assassinations or executions. "Government by the consent of the governed" means that all who are involved ultimately have the disposition of affairs in their own hands, and can make and unmake policies and personnel *without violence*. Representative government is a device to prevent civil wars. If twelve millions of persons vote for one set of officials and policies, and ten millions cast their ballots for an alternative selection, the ten million gracefully concede the victory. A great many lives are thereby saved, as well as much time and treasure. If every national election developed into a civil war, life would soon become intolerable. To this the citizens of Mexico can bear witness!

EQUALITARIANISM AS A SOCIAL POLICY

When considered in connection with the causes of revolution, the appeal of equalitarianism as a social policy is very great. This is the type of notion which is usually thought of as "the democratic idea," or is expressed in some other similarly ambiguous phrase. It is not representative government at all, but is the setting up as an ideal the equalization of property, and of needs, as a general goal of public policy. By equalizing the conditions of persons in any group, an internal stability is given to it which is otherwise unobtainable. Aristotle's doctrine of the middle class, which was worked out by him on the basis of his observations of the Greek cities, is the best statement of this position.

According to Aristotle[4] it is well for men to possess the gifts of fortune in moderation; only those so favored can readily listen to reason. The very rich are prone to grow into great criminals because of the luxury and irresponsibility of their early home and

[4] Aristotle, *Politics*, Bk. IV, ch. 11 (edit. Bekkeri 1295 b).

school life. The very poor, on the other hand, are brutalized by their poverty. The middle class in a society must be large, therefore, or the monstrous appetites of the very rich, and the petty rascalities of the degraded poor will wreck the state. A society should be composed, as far as possible, of equals and similars. The middle class is, in Aristotle's words, "the natural elements of a state." A wise legislator, consequently, always will include the middle class in the government, and will see to it that this class is larger in size than both the extremes combined, at least large enough to dominate the state. He will aim both at the equalization of properties and at moderation in their amount. Furthermore, he will not only watch the possessions of the citizens, but also he will see to it that their desires are equalized. This demands, according to Aristotle, a sufficient education provided by the state.[5]

This doctrine alone would put Aristotle in the class of preëminent social scientists. The way to avoid revolutions within the state, according to him, is to aim at economic and social equality among the citizens. Both before and since the days of Aristotle two-class societies have been notoriously unstable. In our own day the Russian Revolution has demon-

[5] *Ibid.*, Bk. II, ch. 7 (edit. Bekkeri 1266 b).

49

strated again the truth of the ancient doctrine that a middle class is essential to stability. A small predatory aristocracy could not maintain itself in control of the Russian people as a whole when the shock of the World War disrupted its peace-time status. The essentially middle-class states withstood the war much more successfully. No facts could be presented more convincingly than those already well-documented in the archives of history to prove the thesis that a decrease in the relative size of the middle-class in a society is a dangerous symptom. A steady increase in this class, on the other hand, is the best insurance against social instability.

There are, then, two kinds of democracy: (1) The device of representative government, and (2) equalitarianism as a policy of social reform. The first is useful as a technical means of organizing responsibility and of providing for peaceful change. The second is a further means to prevent the stresses and strains which result in revolutions.

Chapter III

LAW AND HUMAN CONDUCT

OUR LEGAL DEVICES are good illustrations of the contention that institutions are ways in which we get things done and are to be tested in terms of their results. The functioning of civil and criminal law and the development of legislation are interesting examples of attempted social control. Legal devices are among the oldest techniques of social engineering.

Law is as difficult to define briefly as is religion, or science, or any other intricate and many-sided aspect of life. The differences of opinion among those who try to define it are sufficient evidence of this. It is not the purpose here to digest deliberately and exhaustively the various definitions of it by lawyers, or by students of jurisprudence, or even by philosophers, but rather to utilize the approach which has been developed above as a basis for understanding legal institutions. What is the position and significance of legal activities in the whole context of human action? Perhaps the divergencies among those who have attempted definition of law are the results of differing emphases.

Definitions of Law

The function of an official in social action has been mentioned in previous pages. An office, as has been indicated, is a center of reorganization, a focus of redistribution, for human energies. One way of looking at law would be to say that it is *the rules which officials have made concerning the activities over which they preside.* This would make the laws primarily a set of administrative rulings and is, of course, a definition familiar in the history of jurisprudence. Law has frequently been defined as *the commands of a superior to an inferior,* whether the superior be an emperor, a king, or a legislative body.

Perhaps the most obvious aspect of all human institutions is their habitual character. Any class of actions must be recurrent, or it cannot be treated by science at all. Habit is, therefore, the key idea of social psychology. Law may be regarded, from this angle of approach, as *a belated statement of the customs of the group.* This is a definition with which anthropologists will agree, since the study of legal institutions at a primitive level, before the development of legislation as an explicit function, conveys a vivid impression of the customary background of all social rules.

Another popular definition of law is this: *the sum*

of court decisions in settling disputes in so far as these affect future disputes. This makes legal rules chiefly matters of court precedent, and is essentially a lawyer's definition.

All of these conceptions are, in fact, interesting methods of stating certain types of emphasis upon different aspects of those rules which are binding in a given community. Indeed, the binding character itself may be used as a differentia. A common factor in many definitions of law is that it is *a body of rules which has binding force.* Even if it be regarded as contractual in origin, merely *an agreed-upon way of acting,* law has a weight, a sanction, behind it, which is felt to give it validity. Almost invariably this validity has been attributed to the origin of the dictum which is being enforced in the particular case. By virtue of their process of manufacture legal enactments have been thought to secure their prescriptive power. These processes of manufacture have varied indefinitely, from the mythical god-given rules of ancient and primitive societies, handed out of the windows of heaven, and the absolute pronouncements of oriental potentates, modern kings by "divine right," or Popes speaking *ex cathedra,* to the enactments of contemporary deliberative assemblies and the decisions and interpretations of enlightened jurists.

Clearly there are two aspects of the problem of law which may be profitably distinguished: (1) What is the general character of law; and (2) What is the ground for the validity, or authority, of the law in any specific case? Beyond these two questions the present discussion does not attempt to go.

The Nature of Law

The character of law becomes less elusive when it is remembered that legal rules have their place within the general body of social activity, that they have to do with the ordering of specific activities. Furthermore, these specific ordered activities may be observed before legal rules affect them, as well as while such rules are being enacted and subsequently enforced. Law may be studied empirically. Jurisprudence is, in fact, essentially an applied science. It is social engineering of a very definite and significant kind.

All will agree that an habitual structure of conduct is not a law; it is a body of action. But when certain uniformities of a body of action are set down in writing, or generally understood, and are *enforced* with reference to future activities, a law has been

54

achieved. Law may be custom, in this sense; but it is customary only in so far as the whole community is interested in enforcing its customs, as these are stated by someone whom custom ordains shall do so. The most basic customs are not enforced at all for the simple reason that it never occurs to anyone to violate them. Law is, in fact, always deliberate in the sense that the prescriptions for conduct, either customary or novel, would not be put into discourse unless the conduct involved were matter for reflection. Hence law has an aim; it represents a deliberate attempt to do something. What does it aim to do?

Human action flows on as a mutually adjusting complex of functions. No law is antecedent to it, but it is antecedent both to law and to all social science. It is simply what it turns out to be at the given time and place. But when, within the total bulk of actions, some are thought to be intolerable and to merit *systematic enforced exclusion* from the whole body of tolerated behavior, criminal law is organized. The excluded actions are called *crimes*. The difference between morality and legality can be stated as the difference between the intangibility and the tangibility of the means used to control action. The community refuses to tolerate burglary and declares it illegal; it enforces this refusal to tolerate by a police force hired to apprehend those violating the explicit legal enactment. The police are but the beginning of a tangible system of officials which operates in this punitive and preventive way. The official function of the prevention of crime becomes as standardized as that of the prevention of fire; both policemen and firemen are on the payrolls of every city.

In affairs of a criminal sort, the aim of a legal enactment is *to eliminate* the variant type of conduct involved. From simple misdemeanors to murder and treason, there is a large range of actions which the community wishes to suppress. It does this by affixing a penalty to the proved performance of the undesired act; and the officials of courts and jails are the machinery by which the total body of the action involved protects itself, in last resort, against the activities which it feels are threatening its welfare.

This is not to say that only by laws are men kept acting as they normally do act. In the sphere of manners are large areas of conduct which are merely convenient, or customary, in a relatively inconsequential sense. It is not good manners to eat peas with a knife. However, no legal rules are enforced concerning the collective observation of good manners. Also in morals there are acts which are judged as right or wrong, good or bad, without being classified legally. The drinking of alcoholic liquors as beverages is an act which has just recently, in the United States, passed into the legal sphere. It is now not merely a matter of manners, or morals, but a matter of law whether or not one should drink. Drinking is illegal. In Europe, by contrast, drink is still primarily a matter of manners. Specific kinds of action may pass into and out of the sphere of legal control, in other words; but the bulk of conduct is always controlled, for the most part, by the unstated and intangible habitual social forces. The example of others, the approval and disapproval discerned in the familiar faces of friends, and other subtle contacts which give a key and cue to action are the most important means of control.

The impotence of the mere infliction of penalties to control conduct was well illustrated by the state of affairs in England at the end of the seventeenth century. There never has been more crime in England than there was at that time, in spite of the fact that almost all offences were punishable by death. A criminal code, however strictly enforced, cannot carry the whole load of directing social action; its very nature is negative, and it is far too superficial, too much a suppression of symptoms instead of a treatment of the disease. It is easy to suppress symptoms; an immersion in ice water will reduce a temperature, but it is not a treatment for typhoid fever or pneumonia. The subtler, personal (family and social) contacts of life give the framework to the culture; they are the leverages which redirect the course of our habits. A criminal code can operate only as a pruning device. It can trim off the activities which have somehow eluded more constructive control.

Even so, criminal law has its educational and constructive side. A penalty which lies ahead of an act is a consequence which must be considered; and the more vivid the impression of the penalty, the greater its effectiveness as a deterrent. The individual man or woman must be made aware of the collective judgments of society, and it is proper that the stimulation be not merely verbal. The penalty is effective, in this sense, in proportion to its ability to call out reflection, to make the individual think before he acts. Here, for example, is an act which the community unqualifiedly condemns and punishes; perhaps there are other bad consequences to the act besides the penalty for it, else why such a bother about it? When a penalty has evoked a deliberative analytic consideration of the consequences of an act it has done all that can be expected of it, indeed more than it frequently accomplishes.

A community can get rid of specific murderers, of course, by killing them in turn; but if that will not keep new murderers from developing, the penalty is not working satisfactorily. The aim is to prevent murders, and the penalty which should be used is the one which will best call out reflection upon the consequences of the act *before* it is entered upon, and which will thereby supplement the other constructive educational forces. What may be the best penalties for various acts which are undesired by modern cultures can be determined only by scientific experimental procedure; and it is evident that they will vary with the fluctuations of general cultural conditions. But unless the bulk of social action is decisively against a particular kind of act, a legal penalizing of it will simply call forth added cleverness on the part of offenders. This is amply illustrated by the activities of smugglers in Colonial America, which refused to acknowledge the validity of import duties levied by an English Parliament, and by the popularity of the "bootlegger" in certain sections of the United States today. Law, to be effective and enforceable, must represent fairly the general drift of social action.

It is easy to be influenced too much by criminal law in thinking about legal systems. Generally speaking, definitions of law have over-emphasized the criminal aspects of it. Civil proceedings are fully as significant, and they furnish a basis of definition which even more clearly supports the contention that law is a form of social engineering. Civil law suggests the definition that *law is a technique of adjusting interests which would otherwise conflict, with a view to achieving the maximum possible realization of human interests.* Whereas criminal law deals primarily with those conflicts which involve what the group regards as "evil intent," in which an intolerable advantage is taken of someone, civil law handles many types of conflict in which there may be no suspicion at all of evil intent, but where adjustment is necessary nevertheless. Courts in general, and both criminal and civil codes, are the result of the realization on the part of the community of the necessity of providing in advance machinery for settling conflicts.

The future reference of the decisions in civil as well as in criminal actions can be illustrated by countless cases. For example, in cases involving railroad employees, or passengers, injured in accidents and bringing suit against the company involved, the tendency in legal decisions is to hold the company responsible for damages. Why not let the loss lie where it fell? Because the company is the party which can prevent future accidents, if that is possible. The assessment of damages against the stockholders of the company in no way imputes criminal intent; the company's purpose is transportation, not mayhem. The insistence upon the indemnification of those accidentally injured is an effort to prevent similar future accidents. If public transportation is to be carried on, let those who undertake to do it take care to make it safe. It is not a matter of "rights," but of the organization of responsibility.

In certain other spheres of legal enactment the dominant aspect of law seems to be informatory. Prescriptions are provided for the doing of certain things, such as marrying or bequeathing property, which, if followed, ensure the protection of the community to the individual in the actions concerned. The rules laid down represent a pooling of common experience and are instructions as to how such matters should be carried on. One does not have to marry or not marry, to bequeath property or not bequeath it, but if one does there are legal ways in which these things may be done. The legal rules aim at providing free and clear channels for the social activities involved. Here, again, law is a means of taking care of a certain body of socially significant action.

When the making of legal rules becomes deliberate, reflective, self-consciously dealing with novel enactments rather than merely reflecting old habits, the term *legislation* may be properly used.

LEGISLATION

Legislation is an attempt to prescribe some of the general conditions of human activity. It is a method of self-direction taken by a large body of social action, and is analogous to deliberation in the particular man or woman. This self-directing character of the community in its legislative activity has been frequently lost to view because of the interrelation of it with the historical fight for political freedom. While trying to steer itself, the community at the same time has had to throw off the oppressive efforts of small predatory groups within itself. For that reason its legislative enactments have frequently been purely negative, and aimed at protecting "rights." As a result, furthermore, the contention has been seriously made, and believed, that the government which governs least is best. But organized legislative activity instead of being aimed at *preventing* something, is an effort on the part of society, *i.e.,* of the total bulk of human activity, to become aware of its own affairs and to deliberate in a certain way concerning them. How far society is to become conscious of this function of self-direction is a matter of conjecture; the social sciences are still in their infancy.

It is beyond doubt that the laws must change when the total cultural conditions shift in a definite manner. When lawlessness develops, a new adjustment of legal arrangements must be devised to fit the circumstances. Arbitrary enforcement of obsolete rules only increases the lawlessness. Rapid social changes must be dealt with by constructive intelligent action in the particular situation. If our legislatures are unable to cope properly with the situations which they confront, and become timid in important affairs and meddlesome in minor matters, it is because of ignorance. Timidity in social affairs is essentially the result of ignorance; and the only cure for social timidity is the development of social science.

THE AUTHORITY OF LAW

The enforcing power behind a criminal or civil code is clearly that of the whole complex of action which supports it. The weight which is felt to be enforcing the execution of a criminal sentence or the decision handed down in a civil suit, is the pressure of the whole body of social action. By that it is not meant that everyone in a social group consciously takes up the attitudes of the judge on the bench. Indeed, the majority of the men and women in the group may not even know that the particular criminal act has been committed or that the particular civil action is pending. But the judge acts in a representative capacity; he is an official of the society concerned. He may use his own private judgment, even as the legislator who votes a tax; indeed, he must do so. But, as the whole of the activity concerned, however oblivious specific portions of it may be, is involved in the payment of the legislator's tax, so the whole body of social action involved gives its power to the judge in his representative capacity. Society will support him in his decisions. In fact the force behind legal rules is the same reservoir of community activity which is involved in moral codes; and no one would think of saying that morals were the command of a sovereign. If one wishes to call the weight of all social forces, as they determine the general trend of activity, by the term "sovereign," there can be no objection; providing it is clear what is meant. When the whole group refuses to tolerate a certain kind of act, it simply is not tolerated; this is true in both morals and law.

If an attempt is made to treat legal institutions *in abstracto,* separated from the body of action which occasions their organization, an erroneous notion of them is inevitable. Traditionally law has been dealt with too frequently in this manner. The Austinian theory, that law is the command of a determinate, sovereign body, habitually obeyed, is but one example of the over-emphasis which can be placed upon the abstract elements in jurisprudence. In an effort to make the application of law deductively simple and obvious it is possible to miss the whole point of its essential nature. Austin isolated the *organ* of the community, and then made it "sovereign" and absolute. But the designation of a determinate body, or the following of any habitual technique of enactment, and the other details of providing the organs for community action, are important only because of the significance of the readjustments at which they *aim.* Legal structures and functions are *organs of the community,* prospective in character, aimed at facilitating certain types of action. If the whole body of social activity be thought of both as the source of legal rules and as the field of their use, it seems obvious that much of the logic-chopping jurisprudence of former days has been outgrown. Law should not be employed as a mathematical schematism, but as an experimental technique. It is social engineering, and should be as enlightened as possible. The test of a law, as of a legal system, is its operation. What are the results? Does it do its business properly? *By means of it does the community reach the goals at which it aims?*

Abundant evidence is available supporting the contention that law has erred in being too abstract and logical. Most of its blunders have derived from this original sin of abstraction. The notorious lag in the laws is one direct consequence. A certain body of rules may satisfy the demands of an age most commendably; abstract jurisprudence then would try to apply it to all subsequent generations as a body of mathematically exact propositions. Its chief method is "interpretation," that perennial vice of the historically-minded verbalist. Antique formulas are clapped on to new situations by "interpretation." The "authority of the law" is appealed to as the theologian appeals to a creed. Legal history is full of analogies to church history.

If an old formula fits the new situation it is an

accident; and success in a lottery is no argument for gambling. There are, of course, enlightened men, who see what is going on and who will make interpretations occasionally which suit their purposes, irrespective of the old meanings. Seventeenth-century English jurisprudence quoted Magna Charta as a charter of civil liberties when, as a matter of fact, it was merely a document granting certain rights to the high lords and barons of the feudal system under the weak and muddle-headed John, who rendered his kingdom in fief to Rome. But Magna Charta was made to serve the purposes of social liberalism by the interpretation. For one such fortunate usage as this, however, legal and social history display many more in which the "dead hand of the past" has cramped the new life rather than liberated it. John Locke's individualism, his insistence that the government keep its hands off rising commercial developments, was liberal enough in the late seventeenth century. It meant the freeing of the English middle classes from the dying grasp of the landed feudal aristocracy which had again asserted itself following 1660. But, transferred to 1900 and into a democratic society, it means that intrenched private interest shall not be subordinated to the public welfare. And this is not liberalism at all. Inevitably the bulk of the historical "interpretations" are conservative; the rules are old, and the situations are new.

If we hold that legislating, all court action, in fact all government is set up by the whole complex of social forces as an *organ* of social action and is to be judged reflectively by the way it functions, if throughout the whole domain of law the question of the past origins of laws and of the causes of events be subordinated to the consideration of the consequences of the decisions to be rendered, a more enlightened jurisprudence will result. Law should be more avowedly *prospective*. All too many of our jurists look upon it as retrospective, as merely a matter of precedent. What would we think of the intelligence of a man who used his memory one hundred per cent of the time and his imagination never! Instead of the method of logical interpretation of supposedly authoritative rules, jurists should employ the experimental methods of the natural scientists. The force which compels obedience is the whole body of social conduct involved, but the factor which gives the laws their *authority,* in the strict sense of the word, is their *consequence in use* upon that total body of social action. These consequences can be determined only by experiment. Laws are like tools; we should use only the ones which do the work required and apply our inventiveness to the manufacture of better ones. The ox-cart or the spoke-shave cannot by any process of "interpretation" be made to facilitate air transportation or television. The view of law should be always toward the future. The *status quo* at which it aims is not that of the past. The ultimate test of law is the kind of future it helps the community to achieve; it is one way of bringing intelligence to bear upon the problems of society.

Chapter IV

INTERNATIONAL CONSOLIDATION

TODAY THE PRIMARY social disorder is international. No problems are so urgent as those of international relations, and one of the important tests of social science is the way in which it approaches this difficult field. A discussion of international law, or of the need for it, is one method of attacking international questions.[1] Formerly an aspiration for an order which gave little evidence of being achievable, international law recently has become a concrete problem, capable of solution.

There are many reasons for the increased interest in international law. The heterogeneity and complexity of human interests is rapidly increasing, while the swelling of populations, the development of commerce and of the means of transportation augment the pressure and the friction involved in every conflict. There is no actual unanimity of attitude among all races of men on most issues; indeed, there is none in any territorial-national group, or even in the local community. But in cities and nation-states the devices are already present to effect

[1] The term "international law" dates from Jeremy Bentham, although the *ius gentium* goes back to ancient times.

enough organization to prevent anarchy. Representative democracy provides a structure by means of which the diversity of opinion and interest is at least prevented from being fatal. The fear of burglary, and of murder, for the most part has passed away in civilized society; the internal organization of a modern state has been so worked out that there are rules, on various levels, which must be obeyed and which, subject to necessary adjustments, are obeyed.

In international affairs this is not the case. There the *bellum omnium contra omnes* is still the order of the day. The present generation cannot forget 1914, and, in spite of all the pious paper-work which has been done since that time, it feels the uneasiness of a group of boy scouts camped on the top of a volcano. Law? Certainly! There is the Hague Court, arbitration treaties without end, and conventions, trade agreements, territorial understandings, as well as such organizations as the Pan-American Union and the League of Nations. But a generation which has smelled the battlefield and seen the vain flow of hot red blood cannot forget the bayonets, the machine guns, the tanks, the airplanes and the poison gases. Among nation-states there are no rules which *must* be obeyed. In every international agreement each state makes "reservations," or feels free to resume, upon short but proper notice, its complete freedom of action—a thing which no burglar or murderer can do in civil society. The ultimate defense of a country is, consequently, still a matter of military force; the appeal to the arbitrament of arms is an ever-present contingency.

It is mere cynicism, however, to say that there is no international law. There is such a thing, of course; but its effectiveness is far from approximating that of the civil and criminal codes of the various national states. The problem of its development is the question of organizing the available means to make it effective and further to enlarge its domain. This is one way of stating the international difficulties of contemporary society.

The Causes of War

A brief analysis of the many possible causes for the use of international violence indicates the tenuous character of international peace today. Any one of the following types of conflict may be involved in the generation of a state of war: (1) *Economic conflicts,* concerning trade, finance, and the control of the sources of raw materials; (2) *Legal and political conflicts, e.g.,* over the interpretation of treaties, contractual relations, territorial boundaries, spheres of influence, and racial minorities; (3) *Sociological conflicts,* involving national animosities, religious hatreds, "insults to honor," and other similar items.

This classification follows the familiar divisions of the social sciences. The underlying biological fact is that *there are separate centers of human energy, and, owing to the growth and development of these centers of activity, conflicts occur at their fringes.* This is a natural, biological, fact—one which poses the problem, however, rather than solves it. For nothing can be deduced from the fact of the naturalness of conflicts. To go on to eulogize violence and war as "natural," because they occur in nature, is as silly as to eulogize typhoid fever because the bacillus which causes it is recognized by medical science. All the evolutionary and biological arguments in favor of war as an institution are fallacious. They need only be applied to the internal affairs of a state to be refuted. Who would advocate the elimination of law and the courts because, forsooth, the struggle among citizens would result in the survival of the fittest and the emergence of a higher type? Gunmen and "hijackers" would survive, instead of the enlightened citizenry. The gain

73

in skill with firearms would not be worth the price paid for it. The same is true on the international level. But the biological arguments for war have been refuted too many times to engage further attention here.

In addition to the subtle complexity of large organizations of human activity, economic, sociological or political, there is also the further complication of spacial remoteness involved in every problem of international affairs. The lack of face-to-face relations makes it easy to be brutal. It is difficult, even in a passion, to desire the death of a man really known at first-hand; the community of interest, merely of a common nature and destiny, if nothing more, is sufficient to soften antagonisms of such a radical sort. But people on the other side of the world, of an intervening ocean, or merely beyond an imaginary line called a frontier, can be disliked heartily, plotted against with a feeling of self-approval, and slaughtered heroically, from time to time, on the battlefield.

Furthermore, animosities and hatreds come to be inculcated by educational means. Children are deliberately taught to be "patriotic" in the fife-and-drum and shoot-if-you-must-this-old-grey-head sense of the word. Habits of suspicion become ingrained, and trivial incidents confirm them into genuine hate, until war comes to justify the suspicions and verify the hatreds. Violence is the method of international adjustment for which men have been and still are being educated.

As special complicating factors in international disputes there are to be noted the small groups which are always present to profit from the use of violence, for example the armament manufacturers, the owners of concessions in desired or disputed territories, and the military classes. The last group has not only an economic and personal interest in the advances in rank and pay which a war brings, but they have also a professional interest in it. Having been educated for war as their social function, military men tend to take the same esthetic interest in it which any group feels for the activity in which it is specially trained. They "make war as a sport," as the phrase goes; military activities are but great international football games played with cannon, tanks, and airplanes. There is great incidental humor in having Army and Navy officials deliberate in international conferences called to consider the advisability of ending war. One might as well expect a conference of Roman Catholic cardinals to deliberate concerning the abolition of the mass, or the brokers on the New York Stock Exchange to recommend the elimination of the "Big Board."

Even the mere habit of national independence has become a contributing factor to the difficulty of organizing permanent peace. Many nations of today have freed themselves from other national powers in times past and still feel, and teach their children, the passion for independence which was developed in the fight for political freedom. This revolutionary zeal for independence of action, for liberty, tends to work at cross-purposes with the attempts at international consolidation. Perhaps this is nowhere more evident than in the United States.

Independence of action, as any other quality of action, is to be judged in terms of its consequences. Obviously one cannot have one's cake and eat it at the same time. To accept a job or position, to contract or be contracted, to join a church, a club, a business corporation, or to marry—any of these participations in conjoint action makes it impossible to maintain complete freedom of action. The commitments which give organized civilized life its character involve reciprocal recognitions and responsibilities. The man with no family, no job, no property and no country may be a free agent, but how pitiful is his existence! The passion for independence can only interfere with the sane solution of international problems; either it must become an intelligent choice of go-it-alone methods, because of the anticipated consequences of such a policy, or it must give way to the intelligent acceptance of international responsibilities.

THE FUTILITY OF WAR

There is nothing in the original nature of man which dooms him to settle either his personal or his international disputes by violence. There is no instinct to war, no antecedent necessity that conflicts which arise shall be settled by the techniques of military strategy. The use of war, therefore, is a means to be judged *in the particular situation* in terms of its consequences. *What will war accomplish as contrasted with alternative courses of procedure?* Here, again, the importance of social science is evident. It should point out clearly the consequences of alternative courses of collective action, including war.

In any concrete situation the declaration of war is usually a gamble for unknown stakes, aiming, as a policy, at some result directly to be achieved by the violence involved. The capture of a city and the levying of an indemnity, the seizure of coal, oil, rubber, or mineral lands to be exploited, and similar objectives, lure politicians into international adventures in violence. In bygone days the indirect and incidental consequences have not always been intolerable; where fighting feudal aristocracies contended among themselves and took the chief consequences themselves, war was never regarded as an unmitigated evil. War has continued in vogue.

The recent advancement of science and the direction of the development of the nation-state have changed war very markedly. The undesirable indirect consequences of it have been multiplied many times over. The means of warfare developed by applied science have become so terrible that, in a conflict of open violence, the damage is so great as to alter for the worse the whole of the society involved. *War today does more harm than good to the total bodies of action concerned.* It weakens all the nation-states which are participants, and settles nothing. The destructive consequences which are sustained more than overbalance the value, to the whole of the action, of any military objective which may be attained. Every nation lost in the late World War; some have estimated that the total cost to the United States alone will run almost one hundred billions of dollars, when all items have been paid.[2] To estimate the exact cost of the war to all the participants would be like attempting to state geological time in terms of years. The amounts are incalculably large. And this economic estimate would take no account of the undesirability of the suffering, disease, and death undergone by the members of the various belligerent populations.

Moreover, the destructive consequences of the last war are nothing compared to the possibilities of the next. Large flights of airplanes can come over cities with ton and two-ton bombs, and drop not only high explosives but poison gas and disease germs. These materials can be handled in quantities large enough to annihilate populations in urban centers at the rate of scores of thousands at a single raid. Every month adds to the possible horrors; it will soon be possible to destroy the populations of both Paris and London in thirty-six hours from a base on the American side of the Atlantic. Even at the present time inconceivable damage is possible between nations in Europe within three hours of a declaration of war.

It is worth remembering, furthermore, that war

[2] On the thirteenth anniversary of the declaration of war the Treasury Department stated the cost had reached $51,400,000,000 (*New York Times*, April 6, 1930).

cannot, by any means, be kept within "gentlemanly" bounds. When faced by the threat of death, whole populations will resort to every means available. If there is another great international conflict it is to be expected that various agreements about gas, explosive bullets, and all the rest, will go by the board immediately. War is violence to the death; and to have been gentlemanly is of no advantage to an exterminated nation.

The development of applied science, therefore, has forced the issue of international organization. Each new gas or engine makes the assured consequences of international war more intolerable in anticipation, in case the last great demonstration should not have been sufficiently cogent to convince the most obdurate. The stupidity or perversity of its future employment becomes the more apparent. What possible objective of British foreign policy, for example, could be worth achievement at the cost of the extermination of the entire population of London? When faced with the definitely increasing disastrous consequences of war, *statesmen of the future who embark upon it as a political means will stand convicted either of gross mental deficiency or of moral perversion.* The bad consequences to the population as a whole have become notorious; either the officials involved will be inexcusably stupid ("cretinous Yahoos," to use a phrase from Shaw), or they will be deliberately sacrificing the welfare of the whole of a large nation to the profit of a small, cruel, but thrifty ruling class. In either case a change of government will become imperative.

But, although it be admitted that war is a means which, given the present state of knowledge, technology, and democratic governmental organization, has become intolerable in use, the fact of conflicts of interest still remains. How are these conflicts to be adjusted?

The Alternative to War

There are means of adjustment available, other than war, for self-conscious, self-governed populations. Deliberative consideration of policy was the method taken to settle internal disputes within the rising national states of the modern period. Why should not deliberation and reflective analysis be employed in international matters? More subtle sorts of force can be brought to bear upon disputants than TNT and poison gas, if the international stage is so set that these other means are available. We are confronted by a problem of cultural reorganization; the web of the habits of men must be untangled and rewoven into new and different patterns.

In order to facilitate reflection in times of international crisis, when hostilities are imminent, there has been advocated recently the system of national referendum on war. In the government of the United States this would amount to a change in the technical means of declaring war. The country could not be placed in a state of war, the Army and Navy could not be set in motion, until the people as a whole, by a nation-wide referendum, had so voted. This suggestion is aimed at allowing the passions of the moment to cool and the horrible possible consequences of hostilities to take effect upon the imaginations of the whole populations involved, in the hope that war will be more frequently avoided. It is the application of the theory of pure democracy to the control of war, and is based upon the assumption that the average citizen will not hate so heartily as does the average official, or be dominated so thoroughly by the strategy of the nation-state. The referendum on war is a way of circumventing the techniques of statecraft as practiced in the nineteenth century. It is both a plausible and possible step in the direction of inhibiting international violence. Its exact utility can be determined only by experiment.

As a means of redirecting the habits of the peoples of the existing nation-states, however, it is extremely important that some existing structure be present, *antecedent* to a specific conflict, in terms of which the necessary adjustments may be made. This is the real value of a League of Nations. Herein lies the value of all governmental structures. A mechanism for peaceful adjustment is essential, if violence is to be avoided. Without genuine organization mankind will revert to a perpetual state of civil war. In comparison to the woes of such a condition the birth throes of the modern state will have been mere nothings.

We stand at a point where the international situation may eventuate in either direction. Either the present international structures will fail and the present populations will continue in a state of international barbarism, or a progressive development of these beginnings will be carried out, and the stability and security of international relations be enhanced. It is a matter of great regret that the government of the United States did not adhere to the League of Nations and play a greater rôle in peace efforts than it has done. Disarmament, of course, is merely negative. It inhibits war, as the referendum probably would do. It can come in a genuine sense, however, only as a consequence of a positive development which renders arming to the teeth internationally unnecessary. Until a *positive* order is achieved, disarmament agreements are but "scraps of paper," incidents in the policies of foreign offices, which tend, moreover, to give international advantage to the government which can cheat the most and "get away with it."

It is well known that had not certain "elder statesmen" of the United States, some of whom were subsequently involved in the notorious Oil Scandal, been so insistent upon preventing American adherence to the League of Nations on partisan grounds, the international situation might have developed otherwise since 1918. On the other hand, had President Wilson been sufficiently far-sighted to take a coalition group of representative American statesmen to Paris with him, thereby maintaining positive contact with all classes of political opinion in the United States, post-war history would have been a different story. While the mismanagement of the post-war situation is a mistake not wholly irretrievable, nevertheless, "there is a tide in the affairs of men," as Shakespeare said, and not to have taken it at the flood necessitates the employment of different means.

There is little to be gained, however, from recriminations and accusations. To try to pick out the villain in the plot is quite as futile as the famous argument as to who caused the World War. The whole practice of nineteenth century statecraft caused it. This is but another way of saying that a total change of atmosphere is necessary before a healthy condition in international affairs is possible. Past events, be it noted, are interesting only in so far as they teach us to avoid the mistakes previously made; there is no one who cannot find, in his own conduct as well as that of others, past errors of judgment, or acts which had been better left undone. The question of social guidance is not *Who was wrong in the past?* but *What shall be the policy of action in the future?* Intelligence is not *retrospective,* but *prospective.* In social matters we frequently study the past not in order to conserve it, but in order to be more thoroughly rid of it.

That an effective organ of the international public must be set up is evident to all thoughtful men. Exactly what structures will best serve the purpose it is difficult to say. Only deliberate experiment can answer that question. The organization of the League of Nations is well known. As a criticism of the present League the contention has been made that an international government in any real sense is impossible without *direct* representation of the various populations of the world in its deliberative assembly. An analogy is found in the federal system of the United States. The Senators of the Federal Government are elected by popular vote; only in the event of death, or of the vacating of an office for some other reason, does a state government appoint a Senator to represent the state in the Federal Government. Furthermore, the Representatives in the House are directly elected. The people, in other words, are directly represented at each political level, municipal, state, and federal. It seems plausible that direct representation would be desirable also in an international organization. Thus the animosities of rival officials in analogous spheres of action would be minimized; each representative would speak directly and specifically for a given group.

The difficult point in all international organizations is to keep the officials of the participating nation-states from using the international structures *merely to further the policies of their own governments or groups of governments.* The ends of an international government resemble those of a nation-state as little as the purposes of the latter resemble those of a municipality. A new type of official must be developed at the international level, one who is free from the prejudices and provincialisms of the nation-state. Elder statesmen are too frequently like the "old dog" in the adage; they do not learn new tricks. For this reason the suggestion of a legislative body directly representing the peoples of the world is worthy of careful consideration. A League which is the football of the politics of the nation-state will not answer the purpose ultimately, however well it may serve as a beginning. Direct representation of the populations involved is aimed at preventing an international government from developing into a ring of exploiters.

It is easy to be too sanguine concerning international organization. Such general shifts of habit do not occur in a day, nor even in a generation. The present nation-state was at least five hundred years in developing from feudal forms. International consolidation need not be five centuries in the making. The fact is that it has a flavor of reality about it today. It is needed, and it has begun. The apoplectic congestion of powers which focus in Washington, London, Paris, and the other occidental capitals, seems destined to be relieved by their being devolved upon other structures. Local government seems likely to receive an increase in its business, and international government probably will be organized to sustain an increasing share of the load. In other words, the nation-state will devolve in both directions, both upward and downward. The integration of trans-national relations, together with the popular understanding of the suicidal futility of international war, makes international consolidation seem inevitable, while the increasing complexities of modern life are forcing urban and regional matters upon the attention of the local communities. We are gradually evolving a world federalism with superimposed levels of social control. The intelligent perception of the consequences of our present archaic political structures is forcing their reorganization.

Chapter V

SITUATIONAL THINKING IN THE
SOCIAL SCIENCES

MR. J. MCKEEN CATTELL has remarked that, so far as scientific psychologists were concerned, America fifty years ago was like Heaven, for not a damned soul was there.[1] If that was true of psychology how much more was it the case in the social sciences; and not only in the United States. Social science throughout the world was a field in which biological, psychological and juristic abstractions vied with philosophical absolutes in running riot. Indeed, only in this generation has the question of scientific method in the social sciences been attacked with an intentness and sobriety aimed at improving such outstanding contributions as those of Comte and Mill. As a result a heritage of abstractions and methodological presuppositions has come down which demands a very careful criticism by current workers in social science.

THE NATURE OF INSTITUTIONS

One of the outstanding problems historically has been that of the nature of social groupings. *The* state, *the* family, *the* church, and other institutions,

[1] *The Scientific Monthly,* XXX (February, 1930), 115.

may be thought of as things which are independent of the activities which make up specific political, domestic, and ecclesiastical affairs. The question of the nature of institutions in human conduct is not easy of solution, to judge from the current disputes; but it must be faced candidly and squarely.

A great amount of the confusion regarding this matter has resulted from the mixing together of at least two problems. The assertions and denials of the reality and personality of the group, or the institution, on one side, and of the reality and independence of the individual, on the other, seem to indicate that the problem of (1) *the nature of the subject-matter of social science* is confused with (2) *the logical question of the relation of the universal and the particular.* Both of these problems are, of course, methodological in character, and it is very important for social science that they be distinguished and solved.

The first of these questions is of such significance that the very existence of social science may be said to be at stake. If no subject-matter can be identified as *social,* then there can be no social science. Can materials be denoted which are social as such? What, precisely, does social science handle?

As indicated in Chapter I, social science deals with

various classes of human activities. Economics, political science, and sociology are interested in certain aspects of the total flow of human action. They mark off a specific portion of the conduct of all of us, and give that material a special and intensive analysis. The institution, or the group, about which the social scientist speaks, is a cross-section of the conduct of many human beings. *The* family is simply the family *affairs* (activities) of human beings, as the state is the political affairs of human beings. To say something about *the* family or *the* state is to make a proposition concerning a class of human activities. The group, or institution, is the *continuum of acts* in a given class, and the individual is the *particular act in that class.* The individual is not the physical, chemical, or biological individual, but the specific act, or nexus of acts, set off against similarly distinguished materials.

The question of whether or not a particular class of activities should be treated separately and intensively is a practical matter of whether or not it is worth while so to classify and to analyze them. That human activities can be classified is not to be doubted and, where the consequences of a class of acts is very important, such as in the reproducing and educating of young, or the protecting of other activities against disruption, an intensive survey of specific sectors of the total complex of human activities is amply rewarded by the predictions and consequent controls which result. There is, therefore, a sphere of knowledge which can be fairly characterized as *social*. To use Mr. Dewey's definition of a "public," mentioned in Chapter I, we can say that there are superimposed publics which are interested in diverse cross-sections of the total flow of human action. The total activity of human beings, however, goes beyond all the distinctions of groups, as institutions, made by social scientists, even as the activities of our original natures exceed the classifications thus far made by the psychologists. Many actions are not institutionalized. Our institutions, consequently, do not *exhaust* us.

The logical question of the relation of the universal to the particular, which is confused with the question of the denoting of the subject matter of social science, has been discussed by philosophers since the days of ancient Greece. Three positions have been taken. (1) The Platonic realistic doctrine held that the universal is the real, that it is prior to the particulars and independent of them. This position is both the philosophical basis and the defense of the fallacy mentioned above. If this notion is stressed as a matter of methodology in social science, it is easy to get the idea of *the* state, or *the* church, as something which is prior to, and independent of, the particular acts which make them up. Since any class of acts is but a portion of the total human activity, and is inevitably studied more or less separately from the rest, it requires but a small additional step in abstraction to fall into this fallacy. The fact that the habitual pattern of the social activities endures through time, while particular persons come and go, is perhaps the chief empirical factor to recommend this fallacious idea to social theorists.

(2) A second position, that of the nominalist, has held that the particulars are real, and that the universals are merely names. If this logical approach to social science be used, a kind of absolute atomism of independent "individuals" results. The individual, thought of as an absolute, self-sufficient unit, who makes up society only by contractual relationships with other similar ultimately independent realities, emerges. This view was particularly useful to advocates of the French Revolution who were interested in undermining the authority of existing institutions, and in organizing, in their place, responsible government. The cause of religious freedom has also utilized this method, as have other movements

aiming at the justification of variant conduct. Opposition to prohibition in the United States, for example, has been carried on in the name of "individual" liberty. If the first view tends to give fixity and absoluteness to habit, this second approach operates to provide justification for, and to confer dignity upon, individual differences.

(3) The middle ground between these extremes is that the universals are neither *before,* nor *after,* but are *in* the things. Universality and particularity are found together. Things are both like and unlike each other; neither similarities nor dissimilarities have existence independent of the things as they are discovered to be. This view, if used in social science, would operate to apotheosize neither the group similarities nor the individual divergencies in conduct.

If we remember that the individual in any social institution is *the particular act* which belongs in the class of conduct under observation, it is easy to avoid falling into the methodological errors of Platonic realism (or of its modern idealistic counterpart) and of extreme nominalism. For example, the family affairs of human beings may be abstracted from the rest of human conduct and studied more or less separately, as we have seen. But they do not, and cannot, exist without their environing and nourishing activities. They are in no substantial sense a separate independent existence, but they form a continuity of specific acts. The individuality of the acts is no more important than their continuity, and neither can be reduced to the other without destroying the utility of the distinctions. Both aspects of these acts are elements to be discussed by a science of the family; but both the common and the variant qualities which social science distinguishes are qualities *of the acts* which, classed together, make up the institution. In other words, these activities which are studied by social science should be handled by a scientific method similar to that which is employed by the biologist and the physicist.

The Experimental Attitude

If we define institutions as continuities of human conduct which are important enough to warrant special treatment, a science of society would be a significant account of the careers of these continuities. How do they move? Under what conditions do they change? What do we find the present state of affairs to be, and what are we going to do about it? The question of the nature of social science is simply the problem of how thought effectively can intervene in the determination of human conduct.

Intervention involves experimentation. In the social sciences there is needed, as a preliminary to such scientific work, an atmosphere of skepticism with reference to the dogmatic formulas of pre-scientific ages. It is more difficult to produce this in social matters than in other scientific fields, but to produce it should be the first aim of scientific social education. We must become suspicious of things which seem obvious, unsatisfied with certainties which are too easy, before the production of something better can be attempted and the means to such production be invented. To be content to rest upon the "isms" of former days is to give up social science and to fall back upon social dogmatisms and creeds. We need a certain suspicious uncertainty. A smug satisfaction with what is will never be the mother of invention, social or otherwise.

But it is not enough to be merely dissatisfied. Unrest and uncertainty may be a condition of scientific advance, but they are no guarantee of it. Dissatisfaction, become habitual, is temperamental pessimism and may issue in the futility of despair. Or it may motivate adherence to various "isms." "Causes" have been, and still are, popular among people of immature intelligence, who follow them to escape the aimless undirectedness of an unsatisfactory life.

Uncritically they set to work upon the program which has captured them in order to escape from the sheer *ennui* of working for nothing at all. Reform movements may degenerate into matters of sporting interest rather than being the righting of great wrongs. The need of redirection, in other words, does not insure its own proper fulfilment.

A sense of direction is useful only when the results of moving in that direction are reflectively sought. We do not need, in other words, uncritical "causes," but we demand ends for our action if it is to be intelligently directed. As intelligence develops, the vague "cause" must give way to specific scientifically envisaged goals of action. We should act not merely to be going somewhere, but to be going one place rather than another.

Ethical considerations are always present, consequently, in social affairs. There is no legitimate divorce of the consideration of ends from that of their means. In social matters we are always choosing between the better and the worse. An ethics which facilitates our choice by importing useful techniques into our predicaments can never be a disadvantage. It is granted, of course, that there are other types of ethics. Absolutistic schemes of values are frequent, and dangerous. When formal they prove too much; where specific they mislead. The categorical imperative of a Kant would validate any conscience; passivism, as a form of ethical absolutism, would leave us at the mercy of every marauder. But all social thinking has had some ethical distinctions involved in it, either pre-scientific or otherwise. Even Machiavelli, whose thought has been usually characterized as having effected a divorce between politics and morals, had his ethical notions. The very seeming unmorality, or immorality, of his thought lay in the absolutism of his ethics. In *The Prince* he placed the preservation of the existing government in the position of *the* supreme value; everything was subordinated to that one aim. The dangers of ethical absolutism were never more beautifully illustrated than in his case. Any ethical absolute, as a matter of fact, tends to be either so formal as to be useless as a guide to action or, if specific, to be positively misleading in certain situations.

The importance of cultivating the experimental attitude becomes more obvious when we recognize that deliberation about social matters can not be thought of as a selection of alternatives which are *ready-made*. In retrospect, of course, the situation seems clearer than at the time of its actual existence;

by a sort of historical fallacy, by reading the conclusions back into the situation, we come to think of the alternatives as having been there clearly defined. But the real difficulty always is that they are not clearly defined. We are in the dark with reference to the ways out of our predicament, and, even when we have cleared it up sufficiently to risk action, the courses of action which we think to be clearly defined will not "stay put." If actions were presented to us with tags labelled "good" and "bad," or "right" and "wrong," how easily our problems could be solved.

If the alternatives were already defined in our moral and social situations then in fact there would be objective rules, or norms, by which we could work. *Morality and social science then would be as mathematically exact and as demonstrable, step by step, as is the science of geometry.* But the real difficulty in moral and social situations is that the rules themselves, upon which the individual may have been proceeding, come into question. In any profound choice, moral in the strict sense, the ready-made habitual courses of action will not do. It is the breakdown or inadequacy of habit, or custom, which generates a problem. For that very reason we are forced to reflect. A man does not kill another man in order to commit evil, or sin, but to "get even," to get money, to protect his life or his family, or "to make the world safe for democracy!" We need, rather than supposedly absolute rules, *a method of analyzing the situation which will present to the individual the relevant consequences of his act.* Hard and fast rules, or too precisely defined alternatives, do not help, and may positively hinder. The alternatives, in any situation, are not ready-made, and we need a method of ascertaining, as precisely as possible, what they are.

Much ethical and social discussion uses the term *value* as a fundamental notion; and then an attempt may be made to classify *values* in terms of their relative importance, ethically speaking. We hear much of "eternal values" and "ultimate values." But this is not very helpful for the simple reason that what is of value in one situation may not be of value in another. In speaking of values, we tend, of course, to think of some kind of situation; for, apart from some predicament, things are not considered at all. Historically the attempts to get a hierarchical scheme of goods, of "values," either turn out to be merely investigations of what it is conventional to say, or end in a vagueness in which no discrimination is possible. An adequate social science will be neither an algebra of society nor a schematism of social "values."

Deliberation is not, we repeat, a process of weighing alternatives which are already formed, given either as qualities of objects, as kinds of experience, or as intuitive truths. Nor is it a process of picking out "values" from any prearranged table of valuables. It is rather the process in which alternatives are *built up,* or *discovered.* Moral expertness in selection of public policies is the essence of social *expertise,* and this assumes the desirability of experimental change. Good government, and good social engineering in general, resolves itself into the question of being as intelligent as possible in the existing situation. The criterion to be applied in the consideration of all social policies and programs is this: *What concrete differences would the specific proposed changes make in the existing order of affairs, and are they desirable?* All other considerations are "academic" and beside the point.

The Doctrine of the Situation

Perhaps the most outstanding critical statement of contemporary scientific experimentalism is that of Mr. John Dewey. The empiricism of this thinker is a wholesome antidote to the abstractions and absolutes of social propaganda and apologetics. He has said much concerning the *situation*.[2] It will be profitable to analyze and illustrate somewhat further what is meant by the term. On page 86 of *The Quest for Certainty* there occurs this passage:

While the traits of experimental inquiry are familiar, so little use has been [made] of them in formulating a theory of knowledge and of mind in relation to nature that a somewhat explicit statement of well known facts is excusable. They exhibit three outstanding characteristics. The first is the obvious one that all experimentation involves *overt* doing, the making of definite changes in the environment or in our relation to it. The second is that experiment is not a random activity but is directed by ideas which have to meet the conditions set by the need of the problem inducing the active inquiry. The third and concluding feature, in which the other two receive their full measure of meaning, is that the outcome of the directed activity is the construction of a new empirical situation in which objects are differently related to one another, and such that the *consequences* of directed operations form the objects that have the property of being *known*.

[2] This analysis of Dewey's doctrine of the situation was read at the joint sessions of eastern and western divisions of the American Philosophical Association, at Columbia University, December 30-31, 1929, under the title "The Doctrine of the Situation and the Method of Social Science." *Cf.* John Dewey, "Qualitative Thought" in *The Symposium,* Vol. I, No. 1, January, 1930.

This passage is quoted to call attention to the iden-tification of "experimental inquiry" with "directed activity" in an "empirical situation." The situation, for Mr. Dewey, is the active predicament in which distinctions come to be made. It is ultimate, in that it is the predicament which it is, and yet ultimately variable, in that no two predicaments are exactly alike. Situations are the stuff of which problems are made.

Let us make a brief analysis of the situation, fol-lowing Dewey's position as closely as possible. Sup-pose we look out of the window.[3] The scenery appears as chance arrangements, independent of mind. If we attempt to make it intelligible, then it may seem chaotic; but *as presented* it is merely non-logical, *i.e.,* the parts are not logically connected. Unless some attempted reasoning is introduced, it is neither orderly nor disorderly. It is just what it is. Perhaps we may see a track with men exercising up and down a race course. The empirical situation, of which this is a sample, is not one of qualities and relations, but of diversified things. Some of the features of the situation are relatively moving; and some are relatively static. This empirical situation never appears in logic; terms and relations appear,

[3] The illustration is Mr. Dewey's.

but the situation can not. The situation, although characterized and identified by diversified features, is not identified with them. It is vague in extent and has no definite, sharp boundaries. The situation shades off spatially, temporally, and qualitatively into the indefinite. The names and terms of language are explicit, but the situation is tacit; it is unexpressed and unexpressible. We may call it something; but now the situation has become another situation. It is that which is not explicit which gives the meaning to that which is explicit. By qualities we mean explicit diversifications of the situation. If one of the men exercising is interested in beating the others running, and is acting with reference to bringing about that outcome, terms and relations will at once come in. The man ahead and himself will be terms, and the tape another one. The time relation will come in; *there is so much distance to go in such and such a time, to overtake the other man.* The relations of the velocities involved are defined in "time" relations. The velocities are already in the situation, be it noted. Extent and movement are just as much qualities of the empirical situation as any other thing, for example, taste or color. We have noted contrasting possible results; one man or another may win. If differing results are possible, we have to choose the elements upon which the results depend. This breaks the situation into factors, and at once we must have relations. *What has been left out becomes expressed in relations.* Suppose an outsider comes in and asks what all this is about. We say, "Those are students out there taking exercise." The given scenes are then contrasted with these same men with books, or in some future situation. Space and time relations are used immediately to connect things. What we call relations in thinking are simply those portions of the empirical situation which are ignored, or left out, in breaking up the singleness of the situation. *Space and time relations are the symbols of reference for thinking of the unity and totality of the empirical situation.* Both relations and qualities are picked out to stand for the elements in the situation expressing the possibility of another situation, either prior or subsequent. Extent and movement have been selected because they are fertile for inference and scientific control.

The following passages from Dewey will make the doctrine even more explicit:

We have seen that situations are precarious and perilous because the persistence of life-activity depends upon the influence which present acts have upon future acts. The continuity of a life-process is secured only as acts performed render the environment favorable to subsequent organic acts. The formal generalized statement of this fact is as follows: The occurrence of problematic and unsettled situations is due to the *characteristic union of the discrete or individual and the continuous or relational.*[4]

Again, a little further on:

In other words, all experienced objects have a double status. They are individualized, consummatory, whether in the way of enjoyment or of suffering. They are also involved in a continuity of interactions and changes, and hence are causes and potential means of later experiences. Because of this dual capacity they become problematic. Immediately and directly they are just what they are; but as transitions and possibilities of later experiences they are uncertain. There is a divided response; part of the organic activity is directed to them for what they immediately are, and part to them as transitive means of other experienced objects. We react to them both as finalities and in preparatory ways, and the two reactions do not harmonize.

This two-fold character of experienced objects is the source of their problematic character. Each of us can recall many occasions when he has been perplexed by disagreement between things directly present and their potential value as signs and means; when he has been torn between absorption in what is now enjoyed and the need of altering it so as to prepare for something

[4] *Quest for Certainty,* p. 234.

likely to come. If we state the point in a formal way, it is signified that there is an incompatibility between the traits of an object in its direct individual and unique nature and those traits that belong to it in its relations or continuities. This incompatibility can be removed only by actions which temporarily reconstruct what is given and constitute a new object having both individuality and the internal coherence of continuity in a series.[5]

Mr. Dewey regards the individuality of specific qualitative diversifications of the situation as primarily esthetic, but these are involved in continuities because of their "transitive" character. This dual character of the diversified things which make up a situation generates the problem and the consequent play of intelligence.

It should be noted that the situation has nothing to do with any idealistic ego-centric predicament. This last is merely a language predicament. Language may be a means in the reconstructing of a given situation as signs are employed in the reflective recasting of action, but language is not constitutive of the situation. It is rather equipment available in the situation, indicating the substitutability of operational processes. Language is the formulas in which we have funded symbolically the stock of anticipations by way of action, the methods of behavior,

[5] *Ibid.,* p. 236.

which we bring to the situations we confront. When applied to any diversification of a situation words indicate the processes expected or intended. Mind does not make its world as the cinematograph projects a picture. Dewey puts it:

The old center was mind knowing by means of an equipment of powers complete within itself, and merely exercised upon an antecedent external material equally complete in itself. The new center is indefinite interactions taking place within a course of nature which is not fixed and complete, but which is capable of direction to new and different results through the mediation of intentional operations. Neither self nor world, neither soul nor nature (in the sense of something isolated and finished in its isolation) is the center, any more than either earth or sun is the absolute center of a single universal and necessary frame of reference. There is a moving whole of interacting parts; a center emerges wherever there is effort to change them in a particular direction.[6]

Dewey has called his position critical radical empiricism. It is naïve realism as well, if that be regarded as the taking of things as they are in scientific experiments. Or the term relativistic naturalism might be applied. Whatever name be used, his viewpoint provides a method of approach which is the epitome of modern scientific procedure. Qual-

[6] *Ibid.*, p. 290.

ities and relations are explicit diversifications *of the situation* in which they occur. All qualities are realized there rather than as absolute properties of independent entities (as in the Greek tradition) or as independent and ultimate *per se*. Nature occurs to us in situations as we attempt its direction. Qualities are in relation in the situation in whatever way they are found to be, covariables functioning on each other, with their relative movements and active possibilities symbolically expressible as statistical correlations. Our discourse is a scaffolding of signs, prospective in character, by means of which one part of the active situation may be effectively brought to bear upon another. By means of it, and other tools, we engineer our way through a world in the making. Our engineering possibilities have as their term only the limitations of organic interaction with the environment; and these themselves may be altered by further engineering.

What is the significance of such a view, in particular for the social sciences? To have made a philosophy of modern scientific experimentalism is no small achievement, one to which the future historian of philosophy will be obliged to give ample reference. Although it is impossible to give adequate criticism of Dewey's view in brief space, there are several advantages following from such a position which may be briefly indicated.

First, it fairly represents the relativity of our commerce with nature. This very emphasis upon the particular situation has been forced upon the different sciences as the most adequate means of dealing with their problems. The decay of Newtonian absolutes within physics itself, as Bridgman's work[7] indicates, has focused attention upon the experimental situation rather than upon supposedly absolute laws. Our knowledge is a function of experiments. Work in biology, in genetics upon the gene, indicates that hosts of factors are blending rather than that absolute laws are operative. In ethics and the social sciences an emphasis upon the experimental uncertainties in the situation is even more to the point in that the contingencies are more obvious. We cope with an indeterminate nature; the situation is an excellent way of stating that fact.

Again, the doctrine of the situation calls attention to the fact that the particular predicament is always the real problem. There are no problems in general. To center attention upon the particular problem is to render a service to its practical solution. We are animals caught in specific actual predicaments.

[7] P. W. Bridgman, *The Logic of Modern Physics.*

Since, on any analysis, we must come back to the particular situation in which action takes place, why not begin there? Indeed, where else would we begin? We deal with nature piecemeal; the situation is an excellent way of stating this also.

A third, perhaps the chief, virtue of the doctrine of the situation is negative in character. Methodologically the emphasis upon the particular predicament does not carry over as a vicious presupposition for subsequent action. Subsequent situations are as experimental as is the present one. It is worth while to dilate upon this point. Supposedly absolute laws, as generalized solutions, do carry over in this fashion. Historically the social thought of one age has all too frequently plagued succeeding generations with formulas worse than useless. Technical philosophy has been a great nuisance in this connection, to which fact such disrepute as it has earned among the members of the intellectual class is largely due.[8] Great ethical and social systems have been constructed upon the immature current science of an age and have been carried on in tradition to befuddle the wits of posterity. The secret of such system-making is out. One takes a favored set of data, treats them as

[8] K. C. Hsiao's *Political Pluralism* illustrates the subtle way in which an absolutistic system, in this case Hegelianism, may hold over into another age.

immediately given, and then reduces or produces everything to those terms. A great appearance of necessity, logical or otherwise, can be imparted to the structure by proper window-dressing. It has been done too frequently, however, to be convincing. The system is constructed, of course, in response to some felt need; but that very fact makes it useless to a posterity with different needs.

The emphasis upon a technique which solves problems, whatever they are, is not open to such a criticism. It takes as its "immediate" only the fact of immediacy. By adopting a critical philosophy which is the embodiment of scientific method rather than a dogmatizing from a few isolated and transitory scientific results we shall not only escape the dangers of our own past, but we shall spare posterity a dubious inheritance as well.

All this is particularly relevant to social affairs. During the past century social knowledge appeared, as we have noted, in large absolutistic systems. The efflorescence of this type of social thinking was in response to the need which was felt; it was evidence of an awakening interest in social matters coupled with a conscious lack of method. In the absence of an adequate scientific technique, dogmatic thinking was the inevitable result of any attempt to deal with public affairs. The systems of Hegel, Comte, Marx and Spencer are but samples from a century overrun with social creeds, dogmatic remedies, and panaceas. This type of dogmatic system-forming is to be understood as the antecedent of a genuine scientific method in social affairs. Under the protection, so to speak, of such inclusive and pretentious formulas, the real intellectual work of experimental analysis may go on. The days of the usefulness of dogmatic system-making, however, are now definitely ended. The impotence of ponderous antique formulas to cope with the mobile factors which are blending in contemporary society is all too apparent. Indeed it can be argued that they never were of any real value. It is open to debate whether social and political theories have not done more harm than good. By virtue of the fact we have mentioned, that the formulas invented are passed on to succeeding generations in terms of whose life they have different, often contradictory, implications, such utilities as they have possessed often have been lost. By a kind of tragic delay social philosophies have become the vogue only when their significances have evaporated. The very notions of revolutionary equalitarianism have become the justification for special privilege. To say this is not to condemn social thinking but to point out the social ineptitude of a pre-scientific age. Where the complexity and mobility of the factors involved are so notable as in social affairs, the supreme danger is doctrinairism. The social faiths which are still in fashion in some quarters are but compensations for the uncertainties occasioned by ignorance. We do not need faith; we need enlightenment. Men have believed too much and too tenaciously. Enlightenment comes not as the result of a subscription to a social creed, but from a scientific analysis of the factors involved in specific situations. The solutions of problems are always *ad hoc*. Only a genuinely scientific method will enable us to steer our way between a sterile conservatism and a futile radicalism.

Take, for example, the problem of the nation-state, that great Leviathan which, it has been said, has become afflicted with apoplexy at the center and anaemia at the extremities. The social philosophies of the last century would tell us at once what to do with it. Individualisms might say that the government should be reduced in scope, should keep hands off, beyond guaranteeing certain minimum "rights," or the operation of a supposed natural law of social justice, *à la* Spencer. The nationalism of a Fichte, or a Hegel, would dictate other policies. Collectiv-

isms or socialisms, would provide still other programs contradictory to those of the individualisms.
But suppose, upon analysis of the situation, it should
turn out that we could relieve the apoplectic congestion of the nation-state in two ways, not only by
devolving functions and powers upon local government, but also by integrating powers and functions
on an international level? Then would we not
want *both* individualism within the borders of the
nation-state *and* collectivism in the handling of
trans-national relations? What then becomes of a
one-way social philosophy?

Even such a problem is too far removed, too methodological, to give much specific guidance in social
matters. "Individualism within the borders of the
nation-state"—what does this mean? Shall water-
power sites be the property of private citizens,
municipal governments, or nation-states? As we
approach concrete detailed action and the need for
specific direction becomes more pressing, the futility
of antecedent doctrinaire systems becomes more apparent. Previous solutions are useful only by way
of furnishing us suggestions by means of which we
may engineer ourselves out of our specific predicaments. Only a detailed analysis of the consequences
of alternative courses of action in the specific sit-

uation can uncover the best course of action to be taken. It is the business of experts to provide such analyses rather than to repeat antique formulas, however valuable those formulas may have been in their own historic contexts. In one situation perhaps an individual should own a water-power site; in another a municipality. In a third, the situation might demand a nation-state as owner; in a fourth, an international structure might be called upon to take legal title. Only the consequences experimentally to be reached can determine which course of action should be pursued in the particular situation. There is no intellectual short-cut by means of which we can avoid the detailed scientific analysis.

The situational emphasis implies that we should keep our methodological processes subordinated to their use, as we would keep tools subordinated to the machines for which they were made. A tool used upon other tools should be even more subordinated —to the uses of the other tools as well as to its own uses. When any tool does more harm than good, we are better off without it.

Politics as Pure Science and as Art

The pure and applied phases of social science should be kept distinct, therefore, as a matter of precision and economy in scientific procedure. The situational emphasis does not mean that the science and the art of politics are identical. Physics and engineering are not to be confused, although both are experimental, or situational, in methodology. In similar fashion the various phases of social science have both their pure and applied aspects.

The techniques of science are pure when they are exclusively cognitive in their aim. Pure knowledge is abstract, in that it aims at other knowledge. If a social experiment is aimed by definition (whatever the ultimate goal or possible utility may be) at finding out how a current pattern of human conduct is organized, and at providing a formula for that body of conduct, then it is pure science. It is strictly analogous to other pure sciences such as physics or biology.

The methods of pure social science, moreover, are essentially those of psychology; human conduct is being described, measured and correlated, and the techniques of contemporary psychology, subject to the improvement which they need, are the only ways of getting directly at the subject-matter. Mathematics[9] will be useful only as it is involved in the

[9] *Cf.* Stuart A. Rice, *Quantitative Methods in Politics;* and Philip S. Florence, *Statistical Method in Economics and Political Science.*

psychological correlations to be worked out; neither social science nor psychology itself can be thought of as a body of pure mathematics. A calculus of society is beyond our reach, however desirable it may seem. But if the experimental method is to be used and accuracy of prediction is to be attempted, there must be a way of *measuring* the results achieved. Economics has such a measurable factor in money. The exactness of some of the work in this science is a direct function of the measurability of the materials it handles. Educational science has seized upon the intelligence test, in the hope that accuracy of measurement of results in this sphere also might be realized. Politics, in the narrow sense, has developed the ballot as a measure of the adequacy of public policies. When all has been said about the inadequacy of the ballot it is probably as successful in political matters as is money in economics. Both money and votes are subject to inflation and artificial control. It is well to remember again that intrinsic values in the absolute sense are nonexistent. There is no human conduct which cannot be engineered into being something different from what it is. But anything which can be measured and statistically formulated in all its processes is the ready material of exact knowledge of some sort.

Pure social science has not only psychological methodology upon which to lean but also the records of history. It utilizes the accounts of previous social patterns and developments, critically treated by historical methods, in an effort more adequately to describe contemporary social structures. Social history, like the "natural history" we formerly heard about, is as important to social science as the latter was to the developing science of biology. "Natural history" gave us our doctrine of biological evolution; social history gives us a knowledge of what has happened by way of legislative, administrative and judicial acts in politics, and of all the multitudinous past performances in our other social structures. What we can plot from the records of the past and the current direct analysis of the living subject-matter, by way of indicating both the character of social patterns and the various directions of their movement, constitutes pure social science. We seek, of course, formulas which will yield accurate predictions and make possible adequate control in the various classes of human conduct. As the experimental method increases in scope, consequently, historical procedure in social science will fall more and more into the background. We are interested not so much in what man has done as what he can be made to do, and, when this latter can be made directly apparent by controlled analysis, the records of the remote past will be of antiquarian interest only. The social science of the future may turn out to be as little interested in the history of Greece and Rome as is contemporary engineering in the building of the Long Walls or of Caesar's bridge. The key to the advancement of social knowledge is the experimental method.

Applied social science is not aimed at finding out about human conduct but at directing it one way rather than another. We utilize our pure science not only by predicting courses of action from observed tendencies but by controlling human conduct. A social policy is a deliberate attempt to maintain or to change a given body of human conduct. *Policies* assume that social actions can be manipulated and outline the way in which that is to be done. They never originate action; they merely redirect it. Present conduct is the means; the definition of an end for such behavior constitutes a policy. Applied social science is, consequently, the art of social engineering. It resembles architecture and the other applied sciences. A statesman is a social architect who skilfully works out his projects to fulfilment.

Not all houses, however, are designed by architects, and unfortunately not all social projects are engineered by statesmen. Social knowledge has a high potential; like anything else which is useful, it may be dangerous in misuse. We have the cheap politician and his propaganda, who confuses the citizen, the stock-jobbing salesman who deceives the investor, and all the other charlatans and mountebanks who practice upon a public they know how to create. All the subtle appeals to prejudice, all the wiles of advertising, may be employed to serve ends utterly worthless. Social malpractice is notorious.

Perhaps we shall never be entirely free from social malpractice. But the solution of this problem lies in the building up of a tradition of statesmanship. In a previous chapter we have mentioned the importance of an ethical tradition in newspaper editing. The development of an habitual punctilious regard for the social consequences of policies on the part of all classes of the socially expert is highly desirable. We need an Hippocratic Oath for our politicians and jurists, and other social leaders, involving a devotion to the welfare of those upon whom they practice. A moral purpose to utilize social *expertise* for social ends must be deliberately inculcated. Mere curiosity may motivate pure science, but only a genuine allegiance to socially constructive ends can motivate great statesmanship.

The Athenian Greeks knew how to state a solution, though in practice their answer to the problem was but transitory. That "spirit of reverence" pervading public acts, that respect for "the reprobation of the general sentiment," that devotion to public ends which Pericles so nobly praised in his Funeral Oration[10] were well known to be the product of education. So also were that knowledge of duty, discipline in its performance and, withal, that subtle discriminating courage which is the basis of liberty, so prized by the Greeks at their best. "It makes no small difference, then, whether we form habits of one kind or of another from our very youth," said Aristotle;[11] "it makes a very great difference, or rather *all* the difference." Elsewhere he said[12] that of all things "that which most contributes to the permanence of constitutions is the adaptation of education to the form of government." The best laws, he adds, will be of no avail unless the young are trained by habit and education in the spirit of the constitution. Men must be taught to fill their

[10] As reported by Thucydides, Book II.
[11] *Ethics,* Book II, Chapter 1, (1103 b 24).
[12] *Politics,* Book V, Chapter 9 (1310 a 13). *Cf.* Book VIII, Chapter 1 (1337 a 10).

respective positions adequately. We build the society of the future in fashioning the conduct of posterity.

If the Athenian Greeks failed in practice at the relatively simple level of social organization in the city-state, what can be said of the possibilities in the complex cultural web of our contemporary society? Today we must educate not only for the simple virtues but for a thousand and one types of expertness. Perhaps we also shall fail; but we have the courage resulting from the scientific triumphs over our natural environment. If we can control nature perhaps we also can control ourselves. There is no alternative but to try. Even our failure would leave some lessons in history to light the path of some future age the equipment of which might prove more adequate. At least we can light a fire, and pass on a torch, as Greece has passed one on to us.

BIBLIOGRAPHICAL NOTE

Those who are approaching the materials of the various chapters for the first time will find the following books, among others, to be useful.

CHAPTER I

Dewey, John, *Human Nature and Conduct,* New York, Holt, 1922.

Edman, Irwin, *Human Traits and Their Social Significance,* Boston, Houghton Mifflin, 1920.

Santayana, George, *Reason in Society* ("The Life of Reason," Vol. II), New York, Scribners (2d ed.), 1922.

Storck, John, *Man and Civilization* (3rd ed.), New York, Harcourt, Brace, 1927.

Wallas, Graham, *Our Social Heritage,* New Haven, Yale University Press, 1921.

CHAPTER II

Burns, C. Delisle, *Democracy,* London, Allen and Unwin, 1929.

Dewey, John, *The Public and its Problems,* New York, Holt, 1927.

Kent, Frank R., *Political Behavior,* New York, Morrow, 1928.

Laski, Harold J., *A Grammar of Politics,* New Haven, Yale University Press, 1925.

—— *Politics,* Philadelphia, Lippincott, 1931.

Lippmann, Walter, *The Phantom Public,* New York, Harcourt, Brace, 1925.

—— *Public Opinion,* New York, Harcourt, Brace, 1922.

Wallas, Graham, *The Great Society,* New York, Macmillan, 1924.

——— *Human Nature in Politics* (3rd ed.), New York, Knopf, 1921.

CHAPTER III

Adams, Brooks, *Centralization in Law,* New York, Macmillan, 1912.

Allen, Carleton K., *Law in the Making,* Oxford, Clarendon Press, 1927.

Carter, J. C., *Law, Its Origin, Growth and Function,* New York, Putnam, 1907.

Gray, John C., *Nature and Sources of the Law,* New York, Macmillan, 1921.

Pound, Roscoe, *Criminal Justice in America,* New York, Holt, 1930.

——— *Philosophy of Law,* New Haven, Yale University Press, 1922.

——— *Law and Morals,* Chapel Hill, University of North Carolina Press, 1924.

——— *Spirit of the Common Law,* Boston, Marshall Jones, 1921.

Vinogradoff, P., *Common Sense in Law,* New York, Holt (Home University Library).

CHAPTER IV

Angell, Norman, *Human Nature and the Peace Problem,* London, Collins, 1925.

Beard, Charles A. (editor), *Whither Mankind,* New York, Longmans, 1928. Chapters VI and VII.

Burns, C. Delisle, *A Short History of International Intercourse,* London, Allen and Unwin, 1924.

Dickinson, G. Lowes, *War: Its Nature, Cause and Cure.* New York, Macmillan, 1923.

Moon, Parker T., *Syllabus on International Relations,* New York, Macmillan, 1925.

CHAPTER V

Baker-Crothers, Hayes, and Hudnut, Ruth A., *The Problems of Citizenship,* New York, Holt, 1924.

Barnes, Harry E. (editor), *The History and Prospects of the Social Sciences,* New York, Knopf, 1925.

Ogburn, William F., and Goldenweiser, Alexander, *The Social Sciences and their Interrelations,* Boston, Houghton Mifflin, 1927.